How to Achieve Superior Teamwork

An Activity Based Team Building Program

by

Louis E. Tagliaferri

Talico Developmental Systems L.C.
4304 Blue Heron Dr.
Ponte Vedra Beach, FL 32082

Table of Contents

Introduction   Page 1

Program Synopsis   Page 3

What Teams Are   Page 5

Unit 1   Group Characteristics   Page 7
Unit 2   Team Characteristics   Page 15
Unit 3   Team Functions   Page 21

How Teams Work   Page 29

Unit 4   Sharing Information   Page 31
Unit 5   Improving Teamwork   Page 41
Unit 6   Leading Teams   Page 53

Tools Teams Need   Page 61

Unit 7   Collecting Data   Page 63
Unit 8   Solving Problems   Page 81
Unit 9   Brainstorming Ideas   Page 91
Unit 10 Conducting Meetings   Page 97

Bibliography   Page 103

Appendix A - Tips for Trainers   Page 105

Appendix B - Presentation Guides   Page 111

Introduction

How to Achieve Superior Teamwork is a facilitator-guided training program that gets directly to the heart of effective team performance. The program provides the reader with the building blocks of superior team interaction using activities, structured feedback and practical application exercises as the principal methods of instruction. It begins with the fundamentals of group dynamics and clearly demonstrates the differences between groups of people and teams. It then guides readers through a step-by-step process for building and strengthening teamwork, distinguishing between ordinary and superior team performance and it gives them the problem solving tools that they need to achieve a competitive edge in their business or industry.

The program consists of ten instructional units divided among three principal modules. In the first module the presentation content is intentionally kept basic and "breezy." Then in the next two modules, the level of complexity gradually increases as the reader gains a better understanding about team concepts. The three principal modules of the program are:

1. What Teams Are

This module is designed to help readers understand what groups and teams are, how they work and what distinguishes teams from ordinary groups. There are three units in this module:.

Group Characteristics
Team Characteristics
Team Functions

2. How Teams Work

This module introduces readers to the basic skill sets required for effective team performance and to demonstrate how teams achieve synergistic results. There are three units in this module:

Sharing Information
Improving Team Performance
Leading Teams

3. Tools Teams Need

The reader is now presented with key techniques that they need to more effectively make decisions and solve problems. There are four units in this module:

Collecting Data
Brainstorming Ideas
Solving Problems
Conducting Meetings

Each module contains all of the presentation guidelines and reader material that are needed either for self-study or for a facilitator-led training program of about 12 hours duration. This includes *Thoughts for Discussion*, a brief overview of the concepts and principles that serve as the basis for each module and each unit and one or more experiential exercises or activities for each unit. All material is designed to facilitate transfer of learning to the reader's job and to provide feedback to the reader about learned principles.

In the Appendix to this book is a section called *Tips for Trainers*, which is designed for training facilitators. If presenting training material is a new experience for the facilitator then it is absolutely essential that he or she read and understand *Tips for Trainers* thoroughly. The success of a facilitator-led version of this training program is very much contingent on how effectively the facilitator can share subject knowledge with students and how skillfully he or she can facilitate the various exercises and activities. Also included in the Appendix are Unit Presentation Guides that offer convenient suggestions for unit delivery.

Note to facilitators: It is recommended that each person in your team building class have a copy of this book. However, permission is granted to educators to photocopy the training activities in this work under the Fair Use for Educational Purposes provisions of United States copyright law.

Program Synopsis

Title: **How Teams Really Work**: An Activity Based Training Program That Build Superior Work Teams

Time: Units require from 60 to 90 minutes. Each individual activity or exercise requires from 30 to 45 minutes. Total time to required conduct the entire program is about 12-14 class hours.

Objective: To provide employees with the task and interpersonal skill tools they need to achieve superior work team performance.

Description: This is an experiential learning program designed to be conducted by managers, supervisors, team leaders or training facilitators. The program consists of three modules with a total of ten units. Each unit is structured around a training activity or exercise that follows a learning progression. Students are advanced from a basic understanding of group dynamics to the mastering and application of techniques that distinguish groups and less effective teams from truly superior teams. They are then acquainted with key tools that teams need in order to accomplish their tasks or to solve assigned problems.

Method: This is a team-based activity. Each team should have from four to six participants.

Material: All of the material that you will need to successfully conduct this program (or any part of it) is contained in this book. Including handouts, tests or other material that must be read and/or completed by program participants. In general, however, you should have available at least one flip chart with felt tipped markers, a marker board with multicolored markers and eraser, note pads with pencils or pens and one or more rolls of masking tape.

Application: This team building program has been specially designed to be suitable for employees at all organizational levels. It is even more ideal for matrix work or project teams that involve both management and non-management level employees together in problem solving activities.

3

1. What Teams Are

Unit 1
Group Characteristics

Thoughts for Discussion

Psychologists have found that most people have strong social and affiliation needs. Because of this, it is inevitable that groups of people form and that most people affiliate with one or more groups. Groups will be found everywhere in our society. People affiliate with churches, civic and fraternal organizations, community action groups, political organizations, hobby clubs, sports organizations, youth groups and every other imaginable type of group. At work the organization as a whole can be considered a group. However, within the organization are many different types of subgroups like departments, work stations, assembly lines, committees and task teams. Because groups are so much a part of our lives, it is unlikely that you can think of anyone you know personally who is not a member of a group or team.

Groups are made up of people who possess individual characteristics and traits. However, the group as an entity often takes on characteristics which are quite different from those of the individuals within the group. Here are some of the distinguishing characteristics that groups have:

Common Purpose: People tend to form groups when there is a common purpose or objective to be accomplished. An example would be a citizen's action group forming to help protect a neighborhood through a "crime watch" program.

Common Attitudes: Members within a group often share a common outlook or have similar interests and values.

Unity: Groups can often accomplish far more than individual members can by virtue of the strength, unity and cohesiveness of their combined effort.

Social Control: Groups develop their own codes or norms of social behavior. They establish a broad range of standards from job performance standards and work quotas to rules governing conduct, customs and ritual.

Structure: Eventually, groups develop their own hierarchy by establishing rank and status within the group.

Affiliation: Membership in groups tends to satisfy an individual's need for affiliation, one of the more important human needs.

Another interesting characteristic of groups is that they can be either formal or informal. Formal groups are usually appointed or elected or formed through consensus (acclamation). Examples of formal groups that often can be found in a community or business are civic action groups, political committees, charitable committees, sports associations, budget review committees, safety committees and company credit unions. This type of group usually has leaders who are appointed or elected. In most cases they share the characteristics described above.

Informal groups are often subgroups within formal groups. For example, a small group of 4 or 6 employees who always sit together at lunch and play cards. Or a small group of employees who resist the introduction of new or improved work methods. Informal groups usually have leaders, also. However, leadership of informal groups is rarely elected or appointed; instead it simply evolves. It is very important to note that for better or worse, informal group leaders can often have more influence on group behavior than formal leaders. Some reasons for this are that often informal group leaders are charismatic, strongly willed or prominent in a way that attracts followers. Informal leaders can also influence others because of special technical knowledge or competence or because they serve in the constructive role of coaches or mentors. Whatever the reason, informal leaders are the dominant person in a particular social group.

Now that you have a better understanding about group dynamics, you should share your knowledge with the members of your class. Here is a short training activity that will help the class understand what groups are and how they work.

Activity 1
Group Characteristics

Title

Esperanto

Purpose

The purpose of this activity is to introduce participants to the concept of teamwork through experiential learning.

Description

Individuals are presented with a list of words in the artificial language Esperanto which they are to match with English words. They then repeat the exercise as a team, this time making a consensus decision.

Time

30 minutes

Resources

Teams of 4 to 6 people each. One copy of Exhibit 1.1 for each participant. One copy of Exhibit 1.2 for the facilitator.

Presentation

1. We strongly recommend that you begin the unit by administering this activity. This will provide class participants with an experiential basis to better understand the principles and concepts that you will present both in this Unit 1 and also in Unit 2.

2. Read the following explanation about Esperanto and then familiarize yourself with Exhibit 1.2. Explain that Esperanto is an artificial language that was developed in the late nineteenth century that is derived from elements that the Romance languages have in common. It was hoped that Esperanto would

eventually become the common language of many countries, thereby helping to minimize cultural misunderstandings. Unfortunately, this objective was never realized. However, even today Esperanto is kept alive in academic circles and, more recently, it is listed among available foreign languages to many users of information highway systems on the Internet.

3. Distribute one copy of Exhibit 1.1 to each participant. Recap the explanation of Esperanto for the group. Then instruct the group to complete the task in Exhibit 1.1 and to mark their choices in the "**Self**" column. Allow 5 minutes for this activity.

4. At the end of 5 minutes halt the activity. Divide the group into teams of 4 to 6 people each. Arrange the teams around separate tables.

5. Tell the teams that they are now to repeat the matching exercise except this time they must reach a team consensus decision for each item. Instruct them to mark their team choice in the "**Team**" column. Allow 15 minutes for this activity.

6. At the end of 15 minutes halt the exercise. Have the teams score their product in the following manner:

   a. Each person on the team is to determine how many items he or she got correct in the "**Self**" column.

   b. Develop an average "**Self**" score for each team by adding the number of correct items for each individual on the team and then dividing the sum by the number of people on the team.

   c. Determine the "**Team**" score for each team by simply adding the number of correct items in the "**Team**" column.

   d. Compare the "**Self**" score and the "**Team**" score for each team. An effective team should have a higher "**Team**" score than their average "**Self**" score. Synergism will have occurred when the "**Team**" score is higher than the highest "**Self**" score of any individual on the team.

e. Optional: For added fun and interest you can list the products of all the teams on a flip chart and determine which is the winning team. The latter will have a combination of the highest score and/or the greatest improvement between their average "**Self**" and their "**Team**" scores.

7. Refer back to the unit presentation guidelines to continue the unit.

Exhibit 1.1 -- The Esperanto Test

Esperanto is an artificial language that was developed in the late nineteenth century. It is derived from the Romance languages and is built upon elements which those languages have in common. English is a Romance language. Below in **Column A** are 12 words in Esperanto. **Column B** has 12 words in English. Your task is to first match the words in **Column A** with those in **Column B** by yourself, without consulting with anyone else. Use the **Self** Column for this task. Your facilitator will then ask you to work with your fellow team members to reach a consensus decision about the match between Columns A and B. Write these matches in the **Team** Column.

Column A	Column B	Self	Team
1. rizo	a. idea	_____	_____
2. peco	b. large	_____	_____
3. bela	c. story	_____	_____
4. kanto	d. floor	_____	_____
5. laudo	e. year	_____	_____
6. granda	f. custom	_____	_____
7. historio	g. praise	_____	_____
8. planko	h. rice	_____	_____
9. jaro	i. song	_____	_____
10. ideo	j. piece	_____	_____
11. kutimo	k. father	_____	_____
12. patro	l. beautiful	_____	_____

Exhibit 1.2 -- Esperanto Test Answers

Esperanto is an artificial language that was developed in the late nineteenth century. The language is derived from the Romance languages and is built upon elements which those languages have in common. It was hoped that Esperanto would eventually become the common language of many countries, thereby helping to minimize or eliminate cultural misunderstandings. Unfortunately, this objective was never realized. However, even today Esperanto is kept alive in academic circles and is listed among the available foreign languages.

Column A	Column B
1. rizo	a. rice
2. peco	b. piece
3. bela	c. beautiful
4. kanto	d. song
5. laudo	e. praise
6. granda	f. large
7. historio	g. story
8. planko	h. floor
9. jaro	I. year
10. ideo	j. idea
11. kutimo	k. custom
12. patro	l. father

Unit 2
Team Characteristics

Thoughts for Discussion

Most people would agree that it is important for each of us to be a productive, competent individual contributor whether at work or off-the-job. The concept of a "fair day's pay" for a "fair day's work" is based on the premise that each of us will use our skills and talents to the best of our ability in whatever task we are assigned. The same holds true in an off-the-job environment like when we are doing volunteer work for a local charity or for our religious organization or when we are participating as members of a fraternal or social organization. But, in today's highly competitive world life is getting tougher for the "loner." It is no longer sufficient just to be a good, solid individual contributor. In order to be successful in our modern world one must also practice effective teamwork.

The term "teamwork" has become very common in both our personal and business lives. Unfortunately, it may suffer from over usage and misusage. A lot of people talk about teamwork, being a team player or being part of a team. Not everyone who uses those terms, though, understands what teamwork really is or how it works. For example, some people think that simply being part of a group means that they are part of a team. But, groups are not necessarily teams. There can be a considerable difference between a team and a group, even though groups and teams may share certain characteristics. People in teams, for example, share a common purpose, common attitudes and a sense of unity. People in a group do not necessarily share those characteristics. In order for a group to be a team there must be something more.

Members of a team are committed to achieve a common goal. They fully share information that is relevant about their task or mission with each other in an open, honest and candid way. All members of a team actively participate in the team's problem solving efforts to the full limit of their individual and collective capabilities.

Team members encourage each other and try to tap the full creative potential of all team members. They have a special sense of team loyalty and cohesiveness. When disagreement or conflict arises they deal with it openly and constructively using problem solving rather than suppression or compromise. Further, team members share responsibility as well as rewards or recognition for their accomplishments.

On the surface you might think that the above description also fits practically any group. But this is not the case. Groups are not necessarily teams. In fact, there can be a very considerable difference between a team and a group even though groups and teams share certain of the same characteristics. Within both groups and teams can be found common purposes, common attitudes, unity, and other characteristics discussed earlier. However, in order for a group of people to be a team there must be something more. Team members share:

Commitment: Members of a team not only have a common purpose but in addition they are mutually committed to achieving a common goal.

Information: They fully share information that is relevant about their task or mission in an open, honest and candid way

Encouragement: Team members encourage each other and try to tap the full creative potential of all their members.

Loyalty: There is a special sense of team loyalty and cohesiveness.

Responsibility: Team members share responsibility as well as rewards or recognition for their accomplishments.

In addition, team members possess the skills necessary to:

Resolve conflict: When disagreement or conflict arises, teams deal with it openly and constructively using problem solving rather than trying to suppress the conflict or to deal with it by compromise.

Solve Problems: Team members are skilled in the use of various technical and nontechnical methods for solving problems.

Make Decisions: Team members use both rational (convergent) and creative (divergent) techniques to make decisions.

It might seem that the above descriptions also fits practically any group. But this is not the case. For example, a group is still a group if there is unresolved conflict among group members or if someone withholds relevant problem solving information from others. But a team cannot function effectively if there is unresolved conflict between team members or if one or more team members withhold relevant information. Nor could a team function effectively if there was a lack of commitment among its members. In order to help clarify this concept consider the following illustration:

> **Group**: The general manager of a business organization appoints three department managers to meet together for the common purpose of finding ways to reduce operating costs. One of the managers heads up sales, another is responsible for operations and the third is in charge of finance. The manager of finance shares the general manager's concern about costs, especially because she is the person who advised the general manager that the sales and operations departments were constantly exceeding their annual budget. The sales manager's position is that sales are better than forecast so there is no need for a cost control program. In fact, he wants to increase the budget for marketing and advertising. The operations manager is very busy with other matters and resents having to take the time to meet over what he opines is much less urgent business.
>
> In the above illustration a **group** of three executives convenes for a common purpose (all three were appointed to meet to study ways to reduce operating costs). However, clearly only one of the three is really committed to achieve that purpose. You can imagine how little real progress toward accomplishing their common goal will be made under those circumstances.
>
> **Team:** The same three people are meeting for the same common purpose. Further, the same basic conditions exist, i.e., the finance manager is very concerned about budget excesses, sales are better than expected and the sales manager is thinking about expanding marketing and advertising activities and the operations manager is very busy with other matters. But now there is a significant difference. Despite their differences of opinion and despite the "weight" of other important matters the three managers recognize that both they and the organization have a common stake – costs must be kept under control so that the organization can be financially healthy, profitable and competitive in its industry. Failure to achieve that goal could directly and negatively impact the three managers. Therefore, all three of them are equally committed to achieve the cost control objective and because of this shared commitment they tackle their assignment as a team – not just as a group.

The importance of this difference is that teams are capable of doing something that is impossible for most groups. While it is true that the product of a group can be superior to the product of the average individuals within the group, only teams can achieve synergy! Synergy occurs when the product of the team is superior to the product of the best individual on the team. In other words, in teams two plus two can equal more than four! This is why effective teamwork is so important to your personal and job success. The modern business organization is built on the concept of teamwork -- everyone within the organization working collaboratively toward a common goal. On the average, Individual contributors, no matter how competent in their personal skill area, will simply not be as successful in these types of organizations unless they also know how to effectively communicate and interact with other members of their work or social team.

Activity 2
Team Characteristics

Title

    Group or Teams?

Purpose

    To help participants distinguish between group and team characteristics.

Description

    Teams of participants make a list of characteristics of groups and teams. They then identify the characteristics that distinguish teams from ordinary groups. This is followed by a facilitator led group discussion of the subject.

Time

    20 minutes

Resources

    Note paper, pencils or pens. Flip chart with pad and marker. Masking tape.

Presentation

1. Before administering this exercise read both *Unit 1 Group Characteristics - Thoughts for Discussion* and *Unit 2 Team Characteristics - Thoughts for Discussion* thoroughly. If necessary read additional materials about the subject to ensure that you, yourself, understand what groups are and what characteristics are shared by groups.

2. Divide the group into teams of 4 to 6 people each. Arrange them around tables where they can discuss the task together. Distribute 2-3 sheets of flip chart paper to each team together with red, blue and black marker pens. Also, make sure that there are note paper and pencils or pens at each table.

19

3. Instruct the teams that they are to make to columns on the flip chart papers, one headed *Group Characteristics* and the other headed *Team Characteristics*. Tell them to first make a list of characteristics that can be found in any group and to record those characteristics in the first column. Next, tell them to make a list of characteristics that can be found in any team. Instruct them to then highlight with one color marker the characteristics that both teams and groups have in common. Finally, tell them to use another color marker to identify and highlight the characteristics that are unique to teams (things that are not characteristic of groups but that are characteristic of teams). Allow 15 minutes for this activity.

4. At the end of 15 minutes halt the activity. Ask the teams at random to read their lists. Use the flip chart to summarize the main characteristics cited by the teams.

5. Lead a brief group discussion about the subject based on key points in both *Unit 1 Group Characteristics - Thoughts for Discussion* and in *Unit 2 Team Characteristics - Thoughts for Discussion*. Ask the class to give you examples from within and outside of your organization that will show that they understand the distinction between groups and teams.

Unit 3
Team Functions

In the work environment teams are often formed for special purposes like solving a technical problem, finding ways to improve customer service or developing a marketing campaign. Other teams might be formed to serve as an interface between an organization and its vendors or customers. The most common team is a work unit team that might consist of all of the employees of a section or unit, like a sales call center team that focuses on a single product or a technical support team that provides customer assistance for certain types of problems. All teams are formed to accomplish specific objectives. In order to do this there are two types of functions that all teams must perform, *task functions and interpersonal functions*. Task functions are those that are directly related to getting the job done, i.e., producing a product, providing a service or solving a problem. They include:

Initiating - This function concerns getting started, defining the issues and understanding or setting objectives and standards of performance.

Planning - The team develops strategies for accomplishing task objectives. It ensures that it has the technical, human and other resources that it will need to do the job properly.

Executing - This is the actual performance of the core tasks of the job or assignment. It could include individual team members operating equipment, interfacing with customers, performing calculations, processing material or many other kinds of activities.

Controlling - In this function team members monitor task performance and ensure that performance standards are being met. If there is a performance problem observed, the team responds to correct it as soon as possible.

Critiquing - Once the job or task has been completed, the team reviews and critiques its own performance. It determines the extent to which performance standards were met or even exceeded and the reasons for those results. The team also develops strategies by which future team performance can be improved.

The second type, interpersonal functions, are those which are necessary to maintain smooth and cooperative relationships among team members. These functions include:

Harmonizing - In this function the focus is on maintaining amiable, constructive relationships between team members and keeping any conflict that arises from creating serious problems.

Gate Keeping - Team members ensure that they fully share all relevant information about the task and that communication among team members is open, candid and honest.

Expressing Feelings - The members of a well-functioning team are sensitive to each other's emotions and feelings. They encourage and welcome candor from all team members.

Modifying - Team members must be willing to change their personal position on an issue when the facts require it.

Encouraging - Each team member must take personal responsibility to encourage the others to fully participate in the team's activities and to share their ideas and opinions.

Consensus Checking - From time to time the team must pause to see what level agreement exists among group members about the problem or decision issue.

Evaluating - The team must periodically critique their own performance both as individual contributors and as a team. If there are any barriers to effective team performance they must be openly discussed and remedied.

Activity 3
Team Functions

Title

Computer Virus!

Purpose

To provide an opportunity for participants to observe and experience the functional responsibilities of teams.

Description

This is a very interesting exercise that confronts both individuals and teams with a situation that tests their personal values, ethics and common sense. The scenario takes place in a typical organization that has the usual policy prohibiting non-work related access and use of the Internet. An employee in a responsible sales/customer service position knows the policy but, like so many employees in so many organizations, ignores it by exchanging e-mail with jokes attached with friends. Then one day the employee learns that the attachment he or she just downloaded may (but also may not) contain a system busting computer virus. What to do? Acknowledge the unauthorized Internet usage to the boss and face a possible career damaging reprimand or hope that there is no virus or, if there is one, that it cannot be traced back to you?

Time

30 minutes

Resources

Note paper, pencils or pens. Flip chart with pad and marker. Masking tape. One copy of the student handout for Unit 3 Team Functions, Thoughts for Discussion, for each member of the class.

Presentation

1. Before administering this exercise read *Unit 3 Team Functions - Thoughts for Discussion* thoroughly. If necessary read additional material about the subject to ensure that you, yourself, understand what groups are and what characteristics are shared by groups.

2. Divide the group into teams of 4 to 6 people each. Arrange them around tables where they can discuss the task together. Make sure that there are note paper and pencils or pens at each table.

3. Distribute one copy of Exhibit 3.1 The Situation for Computer Virus to all team members. Read The Situation to the class aloud. Inform the class that they will benefit from participating in this activity both from a team building perspective and also by having the opportunity to examine their own system of personal values and ethics. Tell them that they will have 10 minutes to discuss the Situation and reach a team decision.

4. Begin the activity and allow the teams the allotted time to work on it. During that time carefully observe the behavior of the various teams, especially with respect to whether they freely communicate with each other, whether there is full participation in the exercise and the way that they process information and use it to reach a decision.

5. At the end of 10 minutes halt the activity. At random select one or more teams and ask a representative from each team to briefly (in 3-5 minutes) present his or her team's findings to the rest of the class. Then, after the selected team(s) has made its presentation lead a brief discussion in which the focus is on personal values and ethics. Relate the opinions expressed during your discussion with the teams to your organization's published code of conduct, behavior and ethics.

6. Distribute one copy of the student handout for *Unit 3 Team Functions - Thoughts for Discussion* to each member of the class.

7. Conduct an activity debriefing in which you call on teams at random and ask them diagnostic questions about their team process during the activity. Refer them to the lists of **task functions** and **interpersonal functions** that are in the handout. Ask them the extent to which they observed any of those functions being performed during their team activity. Share with them any observations that you made about their team process during the activity.

Exhibit 3.1   **Situation for Computer Virus**

You are employed by a major telecommunications industry company in a mid-level sales management position. Your job involves the extensive use of your work station computer to track regional sales data and to liaison with sales and customer service employees throughout the country. Your work station computer is connected to the network server, as are all other work station computers. However, you frequently also store business files in your work station computer's "C" drive for purposes of convenience and privacy -- a privilege that is allowed to employees at your organizational level. At the same time, your company has a rule prohibiting the use of any work station computer for personal reasons including but not limited to non-company related e-mail and non-business related Internet surfing, a rule that has been largely ignored by employees and which in the past has seldom been enforced by the company.

Recently, however, senior management in your company issued a strong warning to all employees that any further personal use of work station computers would result in serious disciplinary action. The warning was prompted by certain indiscretions on the part of management level employees in which the exchange of private e-mail and attachments over the Internet almost resulted in the breach of security about forthcoming company sales initiatives.

Despite senior management's warning, jokes and other inappropriate material continue to be attached to otherwise legitimate e-mail messages. In fact, yesterday you attached a joke to an e-mail that you sent to a friend in Hong Kong and just before you left work you received a reply with still another joke attached, which you downloaded directly into your computer's "C" drive immediately before you shut the computer down.

On the way to work this morning you heard on the car radio that a new delayed action "terminal" computer virus has just been found and that it has spread so rapidly that overnight many computer systems in this country have already become infected. The hidden virus originated in Hong Kong and is spread when infected e-mail attachments are downloaded. You feel your body tense as you think about the e-mail joke that you just downloaded from your friend in Hong Kong. When you boot your work station computer, it goes through a network routine. What if your friend's joke was infected? He would not know because the virus is hidden and delayed.

There may not have been a virus in his attachment but if there was what if it spreads to the entire network of your company when you boot your computer this morning? Should you report the situation to your superior? But, if you do will your career be damaged, especially in view of senior management's recent warning? All of the private e-mail and joke files are still in your "C" drive. What should you do?

2. How Teams Work

Unit 4
Sharing Information

Thoughts for Discussion

In business, industrial and governmental organizations teams exist to make decisions, solve problems and to facilitate (make more effective) the various processes of work. They do this by sharing and processing information and by engaging in an agreed course of action. Communication is mainly the sharing and processing of information. That is why effective communication is so important to successful teamwork. Without effective communication it would not be possible to have effective teamwork.

The kind of information that teams and individual team members may have is almost limitless. Information that is relevant to a work team's mission in a business organization may concern production schedules, customer complaints, engineering design studies, product inventories, sales records, or budget data. In a hospital, information needed by a work team could range from patient admission data, pharmaceutical supplies and laboratory procedures to the condition of the physical facilities, nurse training courses, and community relations programs. In all cases individual team members have information that can and must be shared fully, openly and candidly with other team members and the team must know how to access the information they need that none of them possess.

Once a team gathers and shares the required information they must process or use it to solve a problem or make a decision. In order to do this teams must have two crucial sets of skills: interaction skills and task function skills. Interaction skills are those skills which maintain good, harmonious relations among team members, resolve any conflict or disagreement that may arise and encourage full participation and involvement by all team members in the team's task. Task function skills relate mainly to the method by which the team deals with the information it has available. In other words, the extent that the team uses both rational (scientific) and creative decision making/problem solving methods and techniques.

In the early days of data processing there was a saying often repeated by frustrated recipients of computer generated information: "garbage in . . . garbage out." It means that data output cannot be of greater quality than data input. The saying is still very true. Perhaps it has special meaning when applied to the quality of communication within a team. Effective communication is so crucial to team success that if a team fails to properly share relevant decision making and problem solving information among themselves, or if the team fails to properly process that information there is little likelihood that it will be able to produce quality results.

Here are eight strategies that anyone can use to help improve not only their team communication skills but also their total team member performance.

1. **Think teamwork**. Develop a positive attitude about being a team player. Think in terms of cooperating and collaborating with others. Maintain your skills and competencies as an individual contributor. But, at the same time think about how being an active, effective team participant can benefit you and about what you can do, as a team member, to help and benefit others.

2. **Learn to share information**. This may not be easy -- especially for strong, competent individual contributors who are accustomed to making decisions alone. Information is power. But the real power comes from sharing information, from being an open source of information that helps to empower others. Don't forget, sharing information also means sharing your ideas and suggestions.

3. **Be an open communicator**. This point was discussed in depth in an earlier lesson. However, its importance deserves reinforcement here. Open, honest, candid information sharing is a requisite of effective team communication.

4. **Practice inclusion**. Involve others in the decision making and problem solving process. Passive, one-way communication, no matter how open, minimizes team communication. Some people are more quiet than others. But that does not mean that they do not want to communicate or that they do not want to share information. They may only need encouragement. Actively involve other team members in the team discussion.

5. **Know the subject**. The more you learn and know about the team task or assignment the more likely that you will be interested in participating in team discussions. Subject knowledge will also help to increase your problem solving competencies. People naturally feel more confident and comfortable about speaking up when they can do so from a solid knowledge base.

6.   **Follow a rational process**. Don't try to solve the problem before you have even defined the problem issue. This is often what happens when people do not follow a rational problem solving and decision making process.

7.   **Be Creative**. There are rules and procedures for even the most open-ended creative techniques like brainstorming. The basic concept of creative problem solving is "deferred judgement." This means that at the beginning of the process there is a lot of free wheeling, the generation of many creative ideas. The evaluation of those ideas follows later.

8.   **Review and Critique**. Continuous improvement should be important to all teams. Because communication is such an integral part of team interaction, good team communicators frequently conduct a self-critique to ensure that they are following constructive communication practices. In fact, the entire team should periodically pause and ask themselves how well they are communicating with each other; i.e., how well they are sharing and processing information. They should tackle any communication barriers they might find, just like any other problem.

Being part of a team can be a fun and rewarding experience. Participating with others in decision making and problem solving activities leads to better quality results without sacrificing one's own skills and attributes as a competent individual contributor.

Activity 4
Sharing Information

Title

    Ploughshares

Purpose

To dramatize how the failure to share information among team members can result in competition and confrontation versus collaboration and problem solving.

Description

Teams of participants assume the roles of the supreme leaders of their countries. Two of the countries are belligerents whose fear of each other may interfere with their need to obtain food for their starving populations. The third country, rich with an abundance of food, offers a conditional solution to the other two countries. But, failure to share all relevant information with members of the negotiating team may prevent the parties from engaging in problem solving. As a result old hostilities might lead them to a lose-lose conclusion.

Time

30 minutes

Resources

Three teams of from 4 to 6 people each. Copies of Exhibits 4.1 through 4.3 for all participants. Flip chart with pad and marker.

Presentation

1. Arrange the group into three teams of from 4 to 6 people each. Seat them at separate tables in the same room. Appoint each of the 3 teams as a separate country, X, Y or Z.

2. Distribute the appropriate role sheets (Exhibits) to the teams of each country. Make sure that the group knows exactly which team represents which country.

3. Tell the teams that they are to proceed to deal with the issues raised in their role sheet. Place no restrictions on any of the teams with respect to what they may or may not do as part of their deliberations. But do not offer them any suggestions, either. Do not even suggest that they meet with the representatives of the other countries.

4. Allow the exercise to proceed for 10 minutes. If the teams are still meeting independently halt the exercise at that time. Ask the teams why they are not meeting with representatives of the other countries to deal with their mutual problems. Instruct them to meet as a joint team that has the task of identifying the core problem causing conflict and to negotiate a peaceful solution, if that is possible. If at the end of the first 10 minutes the teams are beginning to negotiate with each other then allow the process to continue for another 15 minutes.

5. At the end of a total of 10 minutes of team meetings halt the activity. Conduct a debriefing in which you learn the extent that the teams were willing to share their deepest concerns with each other openly and candidly. Point out that the objective of the activity was to determine whether there would be an attempt on the part of the country teams to make direct contact with members of the other teams, openly share "team" information and seek a problem solution or whether mutual mistrust would overpower concern for the welfare of their own people. The issue is that failure for teams to share information, the reliance on competition and confrontation and the absence of collaboration and problem solving often lead to lose-lose or win-lose conclusions. Either of the latter materially detracts from team performance.

Exhibit 4.1 -- Country X

You are a member of a committee of equals who are the supreme leaders of Country X. Your country is poor and because of a drought that resulted in a poor harvest this year your people are starving. But you have a large supply of military arms (100 units) mainly because of fear that if you are not strong you will be invaded by your historical enemy, Country Y, which shares your country's borders. Country Y is also a poor country and its people are starving, as well. You are hesitant to acknowledge the main reason for your arms build up because you do not want to appear to be frightened by Country Y's military power.

Country Z, a rich country, shares borders with both your country and with Country Y. It has an abundance of food (300 units) but has no military arms at all, having never been a threat to your country. Country Z offers to exchange 100 units of food (enough to feed the people of your country until next year's crops are harvested) for 50 units of military arms. What should you do?

Exhibit 4.2 -- Country Y

You are a member of a committee of equals who are the supreme leaders of Country Y. Your country is poor and, because of a drought that resulted in a poor harvest this year, your people are starving. But you have a large supply of military arms (100 units). The reason for the large supply of military arms is your fear that if you are not strong you will be invaded by your historical enemy, Country X, which shares your country's borders. Country X is also a poor country and its people are starving, as well. In fact, the leadership of your country is tired of this endless race and would like to negotiate peace with Country X. However, you are hesitant to share this information for fear that Country X will perceive your country as becoming weak.

Country Z, a rich country, shares borders with both your country and with Country Y. It has an abundance of food (300 units) but has no military arms at all, having never been a threat to your country. Country Z offers to exchange 100 units of food (enough to feed the people of your country until next year's crops are harvested) for 50 units of military arms. What should you do?

Exhibit 4.3 -- Country Z

You are a member of a committee of equals who are the supreme leaders of Country Z. Your country shares borders with Countries X and Y, both of which also share borders with each other. Countries X and Y are both poor countries. Because of a serious drought this year in those countries, their crops have failed and their people are starving. However, both countries are historical enemies and they are militarily strong, each fearing that the other will invade it if it does not maintain its strength. Each country has 100 units of military arms.

Your country is rich and you have an abundance of food (300 units). But you have no military arms, not needing them since historically you have been at peace with both countries X and Y. You are concerned, however, that the hostility between Countries X and Y might affect you in the future. You see the current situation as presenting an opportunity to acquire enough arms so that you could become more powerful than either country, thus ensuring the continuation of the peace.

You have recently offered to exchange 100 units of food for 50 units of arms with each of the other two countries. You must now decide what to do if only one of the countries accepts your offer since that would still leave you militarily inferior to the other. At the same time, you might be willing to work with them to seek a better solution for all parties.

40

Unit 5
Improving Teamwork

Thoughts for Discussion

It has long been observed that participation in work related issues can increase employee satisfaction and productivity. However, it has been only recently that definitive work has been done to determine exactly which conditions in the work environment facilitate total quality team performance. The product of this research is that there are six sets of behaviors and practices that are essential in order to ensure optimum team performance:

- Active Listening
- Processing Information
- Inclusion
- Sharing Responsibility
- Solving Problems
- Focusing on Continuous Improvement

Active Listening is a skill in which team members listen to each other in a non-evaluative way, acknowledge another's views and respond to the message sender in a way that shows understanding or empathy and that obtains additional information.

Processing Information is related to Active Listening but also involves ensuring that the team gathers, shares, and processes sufficient, timely and accurate information that is relevant to the work team task.

Inclusion is the process of encouraging and obtaining the active participation of all work team members in the team's decision making and problem solving efforts. It requires ensuring that all of the team's human resources are utilized to the fullest possible level.

Sharing Responsibility is a key empowerment concept. It means that each member of the work team has responsibility to ensure that the team engages in constructive task and interpersonal relations behaviors. It also involves the process of inclusion, ensuring that all team members fully participate in the team activity, and it involves rewards sharing.

Solving Problems is a major reason why work teams exist. In order to do this, they must know, understand and apply systematic problem solving methods including both scientific and creative methods.

Continuous Improvement is necessary in order for teams to achieve total quality performance. Teams do this by continuing to develop their problem solving skills, improving their team interaction processes and by evaluating the extent to which they meet or exceed quality performance goals and objectives.

Activity 5
Improvement Team Performance

Title

Self-Directed Team Assessment

Purpose

The Self - Directed Team Assessment (SDTA) is designed to help members of work teams learn and apply behaviors and practices which will facilitate total quality team performance.

Description

A learning and feedback instrument, the SDTA consists of 30 items with a 5-point rating scale. The instrument measures perceptions about how effectively a work team engages in 6 sets of team performance behaviors, practices and conditions: active listening, inclusion, processing information, sharing responsibility, solving problems and focusing on continuous improvement.

Suitability

All organizational levels.

Scoring

Manually scored. Refer to scoring section at the end of each SDTA questionnaire.

Presentation

1. Instruct the class to assemble in the same teams that they have been in for the first four units of this program. Tell them that the main purpose of this activity is to give them an opportunity to critique how well they have been performing as a team; part of the process of continuous improvement.

2. Distribute one copy of the *Self-Directed Team Assessment* to all team members. Read the instructions aloud and have them follow along in their

copy. Tell them that as they respond to the questionnaire items, they should do so within the context of how well they have been performing as a team in class.

3. Tell the class that they will have 20 minutes to complete the test and that they are to do so individually – not as a team. Begin the test.

4. At the end of 20 minutes halt the test. Refer to the section of the test titled **How To Score It**. Explain the scoring method and provide any assistance that might be required as the teams score the tests.

5. When the tests are scored instruct the teams to discuss the results and share their candid opinion about their team performance with the other members of their team. Allow about 15 minutes for this part of the exercise.

6. At the end of 15 minutes halt the activity. Refer to the Presentation Guidelines for this unit to continue.

Self-Directed Team Assessment

Instructions: Below are six sets of team behaviors that can affect the performance of work teams. Read each item carefully. In the column to the left, enter the value that indicates the extent that you believe the behavior exists within your work team **Now**. Next, enter the value that indicates the improvement **Goal** for each behavior that you believe your work team should establish for the near term future. Use the following scale for your response: 1 = Very Little; 2 = Little; 3 = Some; 4 = Considerable; and 5 = Very Considerable for both the **Now** and **Goal** ratings.

Active Listening -- When a member of our team speaks, other members:

Now   *Goal*

_____ _____   01.   are attentive and show interest in what he or she is saying.

_____ _____   02.   ask questions for the purpose of clarifying what was said.

_____ _____   03.   probe to obtain additional information.

_____ _____   04.   respond in a way that shows empathy or understanding.

_____ _____   05.   listen to what is said before evaluating and judging.

_____ _____   **Totals**

Processing Information -- All of the members of our work team:

Now *Goal*

____ ____   06.   share task related information openly and honestly.

____ ____   07.   provide each other with candid, constructive feedback.

____ ____   08.   evaluate task related information objectively, without bias.

____ ____   09.   ensure that task related information is timely and accurate.

____ ____   10.   focus on factual information -- not speculation.

____ ____   **Totals**

Inclusion – Each member of our work team:

Now   Goal

____ ____   11.   encourages other members to offer their ideas and suggestions.

____ ____   12.   respects the dignity and self-worth of other members.

____ ____   13.   expresses appreciation to other members for their efforts.

____ ____   14.   gives other members a chance to demonstrate their expertise.

____ ____   15.   helps other members participate fully in all team activities.

____ ____   **Totals**

Sharing Responsibility -- Each member of our work team:

Now   *Goal*

____ ____   16.   shares the workload in a fair and equitable manner.

____ ____   17.   takes personal responsibility for achieving quality results.

____ ____   18.   shares the role of leading and facilitating team discussions.

____ ____   19.   helps maintain harmonious relationships among all team members.

____ ____   20.   shares recognition the team receives for its accomplishments.

____ ____   **Totals**

Solving Problems -- When working on a task our team:

Now   *Goal*

_____ _____   21.   focuses on the real problem or decision issue.

_____ _____   22.   follows a systematic problem solving method.

_____ _____   23.   demonstrates effective team interaction skills.

_____ _____   24.   understands and uses creative techniques.

_____ _____   25.   has the technical skills required to deal with the task.

_____ _____   **Totals**

Continuous Improvement -- Our work team:

Now   *Goal*

____ ____   26.   regularly critiques how well it is performing the team task.

____ ____   27.   openly looks for ways by which it can improve its effectiveness.

____ ____   28.   consistently achieves high quality results.

____ ____   29.   places emphasis on continually developing members' skills.

____ ____   30.   is determined to find an even better way to do things.

____ ____   **Totals**

HOW TO SCORE IT

1. Rating scale values are as follows:

    1 = Very Little   3 = Some   5 = Very Considerable
    2 = Little   4 = Considerable

2. Total the **Now** and **Goal** scores for each team skill set. Then average the set scores for all members of your team.

3. Record the average scores for each skill set in the appropriate columns in the scoring template.

4. Determine the variance or difference between the **Now Avg** and the **Goal Avg**. Record the differences in the **Variance** column.

5. Team skill set **Now** average totals less than 20 and/or variances greater than 5 may indicate that the work team is performing below its desired performance level with respect to the relevant behaviors, practices or conditions.

6. Use the team skill set average and variance data to identify the major performance barriers that your work team is experiencing. Then, work as a team to develop strategies to overcome these performance barriers.

SCORING TEMPLATE

Team Skill Set	Now Avg	Goal Avg	Variance
Active Listening	_____	_____	_____
Processing Information	_____	_____	_____
Inclusion	_____	_____	_____
Sharing Responsibility	_____	_____	_____
Solving Problems	_____	_____	_____
Continuous Improvement	_____	_____	_____

Unit 6
Leading Teams

Thoughts for Discussion

Leadership exists whenever one person agrees to follow the direction of another person. But, anyone who has held leadership responsibilities knows that it is not that simple. In fact, leadership involves a complex set of relationships and interdependencies. It is an integral part of the art and practice of managing and supervising and in the final analysis, it depends entirely on the willingness of a follower to accept leadership from a leader. In other words, no matter how a leader tries to lead or what leadership styles he or she might use, there will be no leadership without follower acceptance. When a leader leads, he or she does so on the basis of a power or influence. There are five major powers or influences which most leaders can exercise in order to secure acceptance by followers:

The Power of Fear, Punishment and Reward - Followers usually are rewarded when they satisfactorily comply with the leader's instructions and are punished when they do not. Followers fear the consequences of failing to comply with the leader's instructions or fear the loss of a reward if they do not.

The Power of Tradition - Almost every type of organization, from the military to the church, has a hierarchy of leadership based, in large part, upon appointed or elected authority. It is customary and traditional for employees to follow the instructions of their supervisors and to accept the leadership of people who are formally appointed to positions of authority.

The Power of Charisma - Sometimes leaders lead (for better or worse) partly because they have a dynamic, charismatic personality. It almost is as though there was a magnetism attracting people to follow their leadership. Historical examples of this are Caesar, Alexander the Great, Christ, Gandhi, Hitler, Kennedy and many others.

The Power of Expertise - From time to time each of us agrees to follow the leadership of someone else on the basis of their expertise. When we are ill, we readily follow the advice (leadership) of a doctor and for legal matters that of an attorney. In business, people follow the advice of technical specialists.

The Power of Rational Agreement - Another reason why people follow leaders is because they know, understand and accept that the particular instruction or direction being given by a leader is the correct thing to do in that situation. The leader (or, in some cases, the circumstances themselves) has sufficiently explained the situation so that reasonable people can rationally accept the leader's decision and take the desired course of action.

In many respects being a team leader requires even more skill than being the appointed leader of a regular work group. This is especially true when leading a task team, special purpose team or a problem solving team. The reason is that for these types of teams in particular the team leader is really a facilitator. Facilitation means making something easier. So, the main role of a team facilitator is to help make it easier for the team to accomplish its mission or purpose.

Early studies on the subject of team building leadership tended to concentrate on the personal characteristics and traits of team builders and on their personal leadership styles. Most of these studies were more concerned with what team leadership is rather than how it works; or, more specifically, with what it is that successful team builders do. However, more current research has focused on identifying patterns of behavior that can distinguish the truly successful team builders from those who are less successful. This recent research has led to several important and interesting conclusions. One major finding is that the truly successful team builders place considerable emphasis on transforming employees from groups of individual contributors into highly effective work teams that produce synergistic results. They accomplish this not because of their traits or characteristics, or even because of their particular leadership style. Rather, they are successful team builders because they regularly engage in a set of behaviors that combines a focus on the achievement of performance excellence with a focus on the development of team interaction skills.

Several noted management researchers have found clear patterns of behavior that identify superior, high performing managers and supervisors. In almost all cases, superior managers and supervisors were also superior team builders or team leaders. One of the most persuasive findings is presented by the late Dr. Dennis Kinlaw who described eight key practices clearly distinguish superior team leaders from others.

1.   **ACTION:** The team leader gets things done, solves problems and overcomes organizational obstacles.

2. **PERFORMANCE:** The team leader strives for performance excellence for both self and work team. The team builder ensures that employees know what is expected of them and how well they are meeting those expectations.

3. **IMPROVEMENT:** The team leader continually works with employees as a team to creatively and innovatively identify ways by which improvement can be achieved.

4. **CONTACT:** The team leader maintains open communication with employees and with key people in other work units.

5. **RELATIONSHIPS:** The team leader ensures that harmonious work relationships are maintained with others and constructively resolves conflict.

6. **DEVELOPMENT:** The team leader places emphasis on developing new skills and competencies both for self and for members of the work team.

7. **TEAM INTERACTION:** The team leader is a team player who involves team members in important decision making activities.

8. **PERSONAL CHARACTER:** The team leader sets a personal model of conduct and behavior for employees to follow.

All of the above superior team leader behaviors take place within the context of certain situational variables. Certain tasks are more complex than others, some tasks are of an emergency nature and must be completed with the highest urgency while other tasks, even important ones, might have longer, less urgent time frames for completion. The job knowledge, skills, experience and maturity of task team members often vary as does that of the team leader himself or herself. Because of this there is no one best way to lead all of the time. Rather, the most effective leadership style for a team leader or any other leader depends on the nature of the task, the people and the situation, including time. The skilled and most successful team leader, however, will correctly diagnose the leadership situational variable that he or she is confronted with and then use the powers of influence and patterns of behavior that are most compatible with those variables.

Activity 6
Leading Teams

Title

    Time Capsule

Purpose

    To demonstrate the process by which team decisions are made and to provide an experiential learning situation where team leadership skills can be demonstrated.

Description

    Exercise participants take the role of a cultural preservation committee that has been tasked with selecting objects to be placed in a 100-year time capsule. The objects must represent everyday life in today's society and must fit into the time capsule. Other than that there are no restrictions.

Time

    20 minutes

Resources

    Teams of 4 to 6 people each. One copy of Exhibit 6.1, The Situation, for each member of the class, note pads with pens or pencils, flip chart with marker.

Presentation

1.   Ask for volunteers to form one team of 4 to 6 people. Arrange the seating so that the volunteer team is seated at a table in front of the entire class. Ask the volunteer team to appoint one of its members to serve as team leader. Make sure that the team and the prospective team leader understand that the focal point of this activity is the team leadership behavior of the person whom the team appoints. (If there are no volunteers for the team or if the team cannot appoint a leader then you must make the appointments.)

2. Distribute one copy of the Exhibit 6.1, The Situation for Time Capsule, which includes instructions, to all members of the class. Read the Situation to the class aloud.

3. Begin the activity. During the activity carefully observe the behavior of the team and the team leader.

4. At the end of 20 minutes halt the activity. Ask the volunteer team, including the team leader, to critique the way that the team leader facilitated the team's discussion. Then obtain the critique of other members of the class. Focus on as many of the eight key superior team leader behaviors developed by Dr. Dennis Kinlaw as might be practicable within the time constraints of the activity, i.e., it is likely that there was not sufficient time in the activity for the team leader to demonstrate all of the eight behaviors. Also ask the class what powers of influence the team leader seemed to rely on most and whether he or she varied his or her style of team leadership with respect to team member situational variables.

Exhibit 6.1   **The Situation for Time Capsule**

You are a member of a special committee of a cultural preservation society. Your committee is now meeting to select up to 10 objects that represent the most important aspects of everyday life in today's society. These objects will be placed in a time capsule next week. The time capsule will be buried in a special section of a park in your community and will be opened 100 years later.

The time capsule is in the form of a stainless steel cylinder that measures 10 inches by 22 inches. Accompanying the time capsule is a preservation kit consisting of acid-free tissue and paper that can be used to wrap, cover or insulate objects, Mylar polyester plastic sheet protectors, a sealant for the cap of the capsule and an epoxy-based material that can be used to preserve organic objects like the petal of a leaf.

There is no restriction regarding the nature of the objects that you will be selecting except that they must all fit into the time capsule. You may assume that all objects that your committee might consider are available for the purpose of this project.

3. Tools Teams Need

Unit 7
Collecting Data

Thoughts for Discussion

Imagine trying to solve a serious problem or make a critical decision without having the necessary information. Decision making and problem solving in such a situation would be nothing more than guess work. On the other hand, we seldom have all of the information about a decision issue or a problem that we would like to have. The key is to gather all of the essential information that is available, analyze it and then make a decision based upon the best information that can be developed. This is why data collection is so important; it will enable you to develop as large an essential information base as possible. When this is done you substantially increase your chances of making an accurate analysis of a situation or a problem and of making the best decision to deal with it.

Data is information. There are two kinds of data, facts and perceptions. Data concerning both facts and perceptions should be studied if relevant to the decision issue or problem. However, it is very important to distinguish between a fact and a perception. A fact is a truth. It can always be supported by empirical evidence. Perceptions, on the other hand, are beliefs, attitudes or opinions. Perceptions are the way people look at things. The recorded number of customer complaints about late deliveries in a given month is a fact. But, until proven through analysis and study, the reason why deliveries are late is a perception, i.e., a belief or an opinion.

There are several ways by which information (data) can be collected. Perceptual information is usually collected through the use of survey questionnaires and personal interviews. For example, information about the attitudes and opinions that employees have about their job, organization management, work conditions and other job-related attributes are commonly collected by conducting an employee opinion survey. This same type of information can also be collected by conducting personal interviews with employees individually or in groups, the latter commonly called sensing sessions or focus group interviews. Facts (factual information) can also be obtained from questionnaires. Information about a person's education, work experience and job knowledge, for example, can be obtained through the use of questionnaires and tests. Other methods for collecting factual information include observation, records research, statistical studies, instrument measurement and through the process of sampling.

Teams need timely, accurate and reliable data in order to successfully perform their assigned tasks and to accomplish their objectives or purpose. Work teams need a continuous flow of data in order to produce a product or provide a service at the required levels of quantity and quality. Special purpose teams and task teams need the levels of information to identify and solve problems or to make the best decision. When the required information is collected, it must be openly shared among members of the team and processed among them. It must be displayed in a way that it can be understood, analyzed and used as the team collaborates to make decisions and solve problems. A common way to display data is by using charts and graphs. Among the more useful types of charts and graphs are bar charts, line graphs, pie charts and histograms.

Bar Charts are usually used to show a comparison of data. Figure 1, for example, is a bar chart that compares the number of service calls per calendar quarter that four field teams made during a year. Histograms are bar charts that display data time units like months or years.

Figure 1

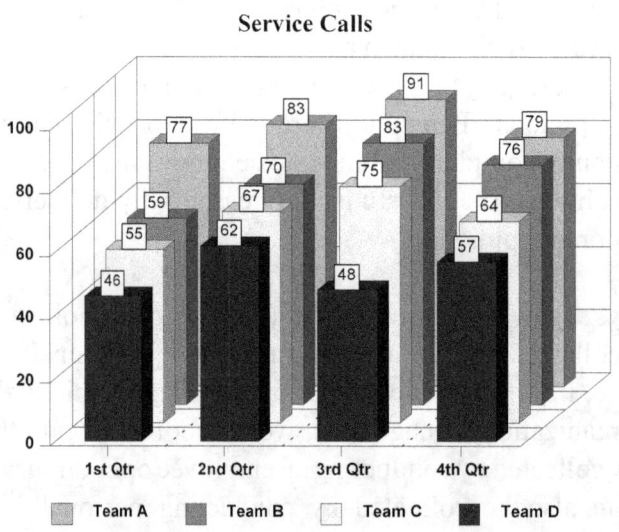

When you construct a bar chart be sure to record or list quantities produced or quality levels on the Y Axis, the vertical axis on the left side of the chart. The X Axis, the horizontal line at the bottom of the chart, usually lists information such as time, duration, operator numbers, machine numbers and shifts.

Line Graphs can sometimes be used to show trends and patterns more effectively than bar charts. A line graph depicts the same kind of data that is listed in bar charts. However, instead of using a bar to show a comparison of data, points are plotted to correspond with the data and lines are then used to connect the points. In order to illustrate this attribute of line graphs Figure 2 depicts the same information as in Figure 1 above.

Figure 2

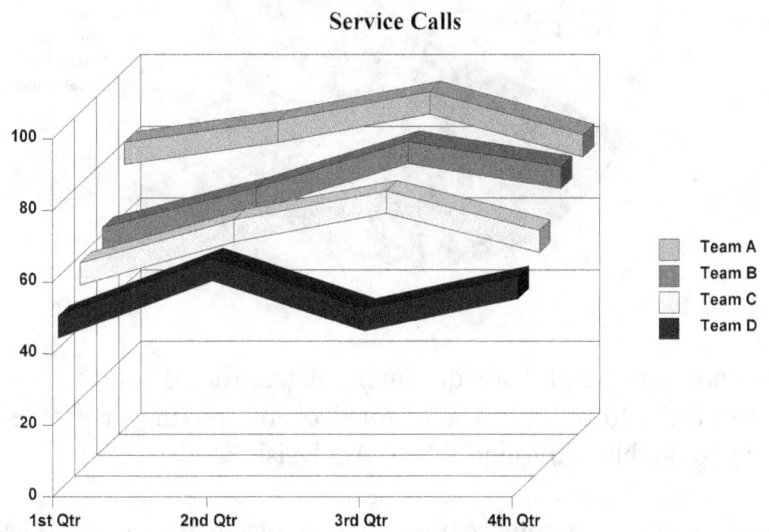

Pie Charts are so called because of their circular shape and because their sections resemble the slices of a pie. Pie charts are especially useful for dramatizing the relationship between one part and another. Figure 3 shows a pie chart depicting the relationship and magnitude of costs for a certain project.

Figure 3

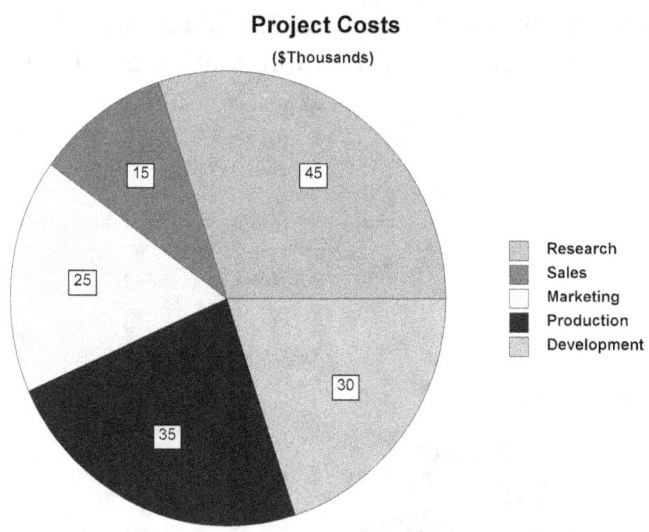

Charts and graphs are very helpful for displaying data. But, displayed data must be further processed in order to be fully useful for decision making or problem solving purposes. One way to do this is through Pareto Analysis.

In the late 1800's an Italian economist, Alfredo Pareto, discovered a remarkable natural phenomenon. Pareto observed that in financial matters 80% of outcomes resulted from only 20% of the causes. For example, 20% of a person's investment portfolio usually produced 80% of the profits. Remarkably, this observation holds true for things in nature, also. If you cut a tree down and look at the cross-section you have just cut you see the tree's growth rings. Study the stump carefully and you will observe 80% of the rings are contained in 20% of the area of the cross-section. Within the universe 80% of a galaxy's stars can be found in 20% of the space that the galaxy occupies. The chambers of the Nautilus, a crustacean, follow this interesting ratio as do parts and components of almost all matter.

No one knows what the significance of this natural law is. We do know that it exists throughout all of nature and that it affects us in many ways. For example, here are some "80% - 20%" observations about people and things that seem to regularly occur in the work place:

66

- 80% of all absenteeism and accidents can usually be traced to 20% of the employees.

- 80% of machine downtime is usually caused by 20% of the machines.

- 80% of a company's profits usually come from 20% of its product line.

- 80% of costs involved in producing a product or service can usually be traced to only 20% of the cost elements.

This ratio exists <u>before</u> any attempt is made to change a condition where the 80/20 rule can be found. After change is effected this ratio no longer holds constant.

This interesting phenomenon has important implications for problem solving. For example, suppose we have a quality problem concerning the production of defective parts. If we know that 80% of defective work can probably be traced to only 20% of the work stations we can analyze what is occurring at those stations very carefully. If the conditions causing defects at those work stations are corrected, we will achieve a dramatic improvement in overall product quality!

The most common way to use the Pareto principle is to construct a Pareto distribution table and analyze the data that it presents. Figure 4 shows a Pareto distribution based on a summary of the types of customer complaints during January for a health care insurance provider call center. The complaints have been listed in order of frequency. Note that three or 20% of the fifteen complaints account for 78.1% of the total number of complaints during January. Remedial problem solving focusing on reducing customer complaints, therefore, should obviously concentrate on those three complaint types first.

Figure 4

Customer Complaint Analysis - January		
Complaint	Number	Cum.%
Slow Claims processing	88	43.7
Long wait to speak with "human" on a telephone	47	67.2
Customer service representative lacks policy knowledge	22	78.1
Failure to pay doctor/hospital in timely way	13	84.5
Internet account access problems	6	87.5
Account posting error	5	90.0
Incorrect premium charge	4	92.0
Benefits calculation error	3	93.5
Benefit plan difficult to understand	3	95.0
Discourteous customer service representative	3	96.5
Uncompetitive premium rates	2	97.5
Failure of customer service representative to return call	2	98.5
Call center telephone menu confusing	1	99.0
Benefits statement difficult to understand	1	99.5
Poor plan coverage	1	100
Total	201	

Collecting data, displaying it in the form of charts, graphs and tables and analyzing data to find trends and patterns of significance are crucial skills that should be learned by all members of a work team. There are many other ways to collect and analyze data such as sampling methods, the preparation and use of control charts, scattergrams and other techniques that are useful in certain applications. Those methods and techniques are not, however, within the scope of this program. Nonetheless, the data collection and analysis techniques presented in this unit have been carefully selected so that they can be readily understood and easily applied by any employee who is seeking to improve his or her performance as a member of a work team.

Activity 7
Collecting Data

Title

Information Overload

Purpose

To help participants develop skill in collecting and processing data that is relevant to a work problem.

Description

Participants take the role of a task team that is trying to identify the most serious issues that seem to be affecting customer satisfaction. However, they are overwhelmed with data from a variety of sources and must first separate the unimportant issues from those that truly impact the real problem. In order to do this they must construct several charts and graphs.

Time

45 minutes

Resources

Three teams of from 4 to 6 people each. Copies of Exhibits 7.1 through 7.8 for all participants. Flip chart with pad and marker. At least one electronic calculator per team and a supply of engineering chart paper.

Presentation

1.   This activity will likely prove to be the most difficult in the program for both your students and for you. Therefore, very thorough preparation is recommended. Begin by dividing the class into teams of from 4 to 6 people each and have them seated comfortably at tables. Make sure that you have distributed the chart paper and other paper supplies to them.

2. Explain to the class that the purpose of this activity is to provide them with an opportunity to practice processing data, especially with respect to converting raw data into a display form such as a chart, graph or table that more effectively facilitates data analysis.

3, Distribute one copy of Exhibit 7.1 to all members of the class. Read The Situation aloud and ask the class to follow along on their copies as you read. Ensure that they understand that they are taking the role of the Wasselworth enterprises task team that is assigned to help management identify problems that might be affecting the quality of customer service. Tell them that because of the time allowed for the activity they will deal with only a small amount of the data that is being collected.

4. Distribute one copy of Exhibits 7.2 through 7.5 to all members of the class. Inform them that the exhibits are in the form of E-Memos addressed to the task team. Tell the class that just like actual on the job situations the data that is available to them in this activity is not presented in the ideal way. That is, the teams must sift through the data and then arrange it in a way that is more useful for analysis purposes. This means that they must convert the raw data to better visual forms like charts, graphs or tables. Ensure that they understand that it is up to them to choose the display methods that they feel will be best for any particular set of data.

5. Begin the activity. Allow it to proceed for 20 minutes. If necessary you may add another 10 minutes. But, no later than after 30 minutes halt the activity and ask the teams at random to explain and show how they displayed the data that was contained in the exhibits.

6. Conduct a brief review about data collection, charts, graphs, and tables. Then distribute copies of Exhibits 6 through 9 to the class. Review the charts and graphs that are provided and relate them to those prepared by the class. Point out that the data could have been presented using other styles of charts or graphs but the ones in Exhibits 6 through 9 are illustrations of how the data in the E-Memos could be properly displayed.

Exhibit 7.1

The Situation

Wasselworth Enterprises is a shipping and distribution center that has contracted with several E-Business companies to provide fulfillment services for their respective product lines. Customer orders are electronically sent to Wasselworth by its commercial accounts whenever a retail customer places a telephone or Internet order with the latter. Wasselworth maintains product inventories for its customers, prepares shipping invoices, packages the retail customers' orders and ships the orders to them via either standard ground or air express means, depending on the retail customer's preferences.

This past year Wasselworth moved into a new facility that was designed to have state-of-the-art handling equipment. Unfortunately, many problems have developed with Wasselworth's distribution system since the move and Wasselworth finds itself on the brink of losing more than one of its key accounts. Wasselworth's senior management has decided that the best way to deal with the situation is to form a special task team consisting of both management and non-management employees from various departments of the organization. The purpose of the task team is to help management focus in on problems within the organization that might be adversely affecting its ability to properly serve its accounts. You have been appointed to this task team.

The task team is now meeting to sift through some of the preliminary data that it has collected from various department supervisors. Your team must sift through the data for information that may be relevant to the problem situation. In order to help you do this you have agreed to display the data that you select in the form of charts and graphs. It is up to your team to decide what data to select and how to display it.

Exhibit 7.2

E-Memo

To: Task Team
Fm: P. Hadley, Packaging

This is in response to your request for information about problems that my department has found with orders sent to us for packing. Let me give you this example of the problem that we have been dealing with. December was a heavy month because of the holidays. But, let's take one small commercial account as an illustration - International Yogle. We packed 1,265 orders for them. Twenty-two percent of them, that's 278 orders, had problems of one sort or another. Eighty-seven orders were missing packing slips, 49 had the wrong product, 75 were damaged before they got here, 30 were missing instruction manuals and the balance of the problems you cold group under "miscellaneous, " including 18 that quality control had marked defective. Now how are we supposed to provide quality customer service under those circumstances?

Exhibit 7.3

E-Memo

To: Task Team
Fm: A. Holder, Bldg.15

Thank you for asking me to send you information about the inventory problem that we have been having. **At last someone is listening!** Anyway, the following is a list of products that have had the greatest shortages, meaning that we run out of them most frequently. All figures are for year-to-date.

Product Code	Nr. Shortages
N5478	23
R9821C	56
M3000	17
N5471C	60
N5502	49
R8756	78
M3002	11
C2500L	31
N5480	9
R1600	7
R1606	11
M4050	19
A2344	8
A2345	6
S2123	9
M4330	29
C2565L	53
N5600B	14
C380	5
B1111	7

Now, let's hope that you can do something about it!

Exhibit 7.4

E-Memo

To: Task Team
Fm: C. Wasselworth, Sales

You asked me to send you statistics about the number of complaints that we get from key accounts. I did an analysis by sales region so I will present it to you that way.

In October we got 33 complaints from Region 1, 15 from Region 2, 20 from Region 5, 11 from Region 3 and another 13 from Region 4. Then in November it was 10 from Region 5, 8 from Region 4, 16 from Region 2 and Region 3 had 12. Oh yes, in November there were also 9 from Region 1. Lastly, in December it was Region 1-26, Region 2-3, Region 3-2, Region 4-15 and Region 5 had only 4.

Let me know if you need anything else.

Exhibit 7.5

E-Memo

To: Task Team
Fm: R. Garcia

I am responding to your request for a breakdown of annual revenue from our five largest commercial accounts. All revenue is in thousands of dollars.

Macrotonic	$732
Lodlow	$116
Zork	$475
Middleton	$296
Express	$350

Exhibit 7.6

Suggested Bar Chart for Exhibit 7.2

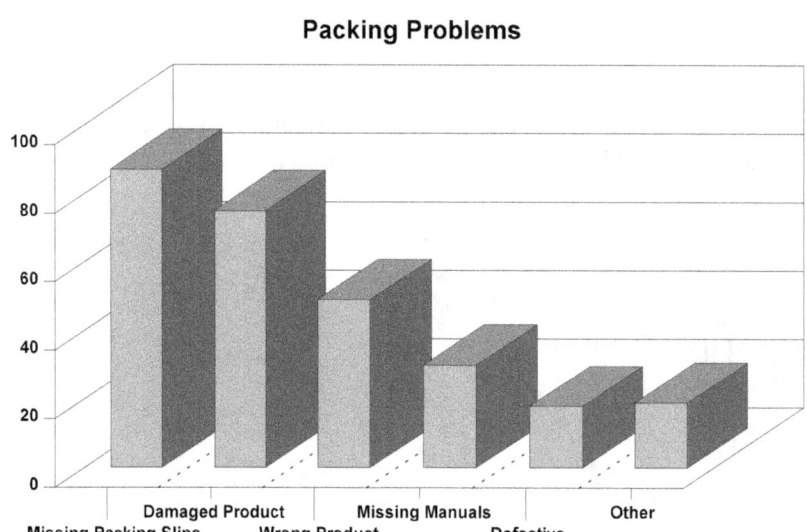

Exhibit 7.7

Suggested Pareto Table for Exhibit 7.3

Inventory Shortages		
Product Code	**Nr. Shortages**	**Cum. %**
R8756	178	32.4
N5471C	120	54.2
R9821C	76	68.0
C2565L	68	80.3
N5502	29	85.6
C2500L	21	87.8
M4330	12	89.6
N5478	10	93.4
M4050	8	94.9
M3000	5	95.8
N5600B	4	96.5
M3002	4	97.2
R1606	3	97.8
N5480	3	98.3
S2123	3	98.7
A2344	2	99.0
R1600	1	99.4
B1111	1	99.6
A2345	1	99.8
C380	1	100
Total	550	

Exhibit 7.8

Suggested Line Graph for Exhibit 7.4

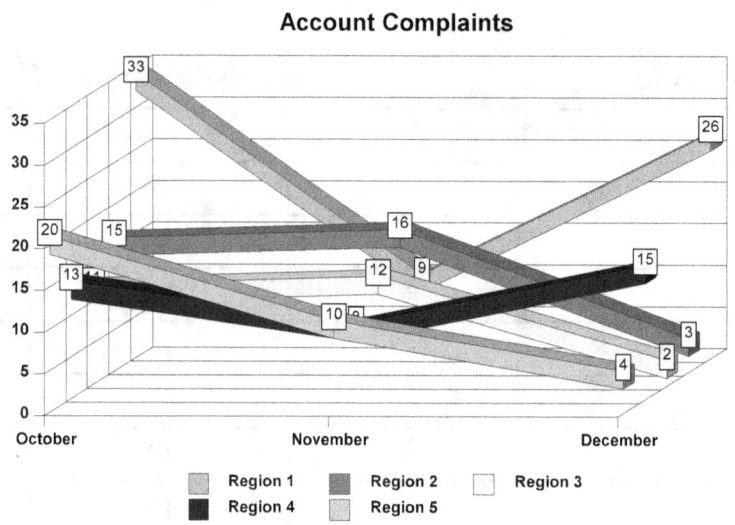

Account Complaints

Exhibit 7.9

Suggested Pie Chart for Exhibit 7.5

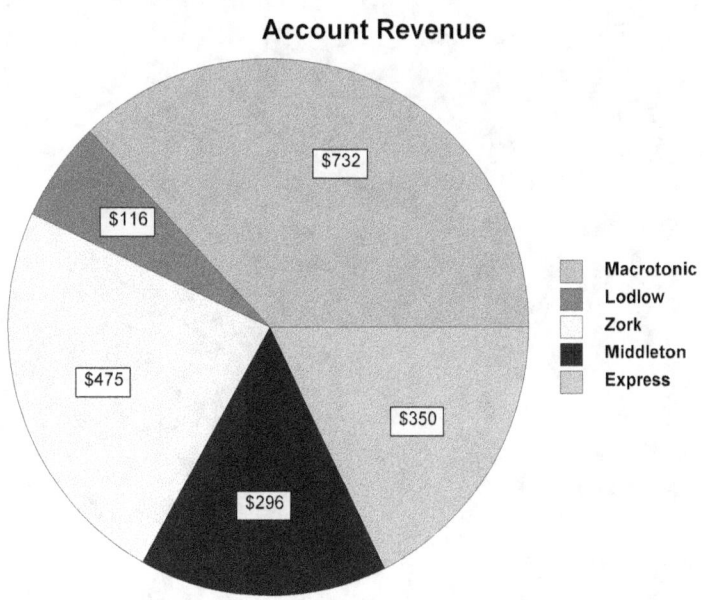

Unit 8
Solving Problems

Thoughts for Discussion

One of the most important responsibilities of employees and of teams is to solve problems. Individual employees continuously are required to solve technical, administrative, sales, and customer service problems that arise within their areas of responsibility. Work groups and task teams must solve production, quality, productivity, morale and other problems. Managers, supervisors and other work group leaders must not only facilitate effective problem-solving within their work groups but in addition must occasionally resolve interpersonal conflict and employee performance problems.

All problem solving requires that a decision be made. The process or method by which problems are solved and by which decisions are made is very similar. Because of this, good problem solvers are also usually good decision makers. Unfortunately, less than 50% of all managers, supervisors and other work group leaders are good problem solvers. The reason for this is that less than 50% of these leaders use a systematic method when solving a problem. Many proprietary problem solving systems have been developed in order to help leaders and individual employees improve their problem solving skills. Some are very easy to use while others are more complicated. However, almost all of them follow these basic systematic steps:

1. **Define the Problem**

    Failure to accurately define or determine the real problem or decision issue is a major reason why many problem solving efforts are ineffective. In order to overcome this barrier it is necessary to distinguish between a symptom and the true nature of the problem. In most cases this can be done by first writing a general description of the overall problem situation. Then break the "fuzzy" problem situation into its components and look for the component that seems to be the primary basis for all of the other components.

2. **Gather the Facts**

    Before a problem can be rationally tackled, the facts about it must be known. In some cases, especially with technical problems like those related to quality improvement, it is possible to gather problem related facts by using data collection aids like charts and graphs (process flow charts, histograms, control charts, etc.). In other cases information can be collected through personal observation, employee records, personal interviews and by asking diagnostic questions like how, what, when, where, why, how much, how fast, and so on. The accuracy of your problem solving efforts depends to a large extent on how much accurate information you have about the problem.

3.   **Analyze the Problem**

Problems are usually variances from desired outcomes. In order to understand the variance, it is first necessary to clearly understand what should happen and also what is happening. The difference between what should happen and what is happening is the variance or problem. The next step is to determine why the variance occurred. This means looking for the problem root cause -- again, not for its symptoms. There are several useful techniques like cause-effect diagraming that help identify problem root causes, but a very simple aid is the "why" technique. This method begins with the clearly defined variance or precisely stated problem. The sequence of "why" technique questions can best be illustrated by an example in which the problem or variance was found to be:

> "Response time to customer inquiries about the status of their orders now averages 3 hours. The best employees respond with 30 minutes and the standard for response time is 1 hour."

> **Why is the average response time 3 hours?**

> "Because there are many new, inexperienced employees in the customer service section."

>> **Why are there many new, inexperienced employees ...."**

>> "Because many of the more experience employees have left the company."

>> **Why have many of the more experienced ...."**

>> Because they felt that they had little control over their job and that no one was interested in their opinions."

Why did they feel ....

Obviously, the example is leading in a direction that would probably indicate weak leadership in the customer service section, failure to listen to employees' problems and concerns, an absence of empowerment, etc. Note that there may be more than one answer to the initial "why" question and that response would have to be followed using the "why" technique, also.

4.   **Develop Alternative Solutions**

Once the root cause of the problem has been identified, alternative solutions must be developed. One effective and easy-to-use method to do this is through brainstorming. Brainstorming is a technique in which the objective is to develop as many alternative solutions as possible in a short period of time. The key is to make a written list of ideas without pausing to evaluate, make judgements, or asking questions for the purpose of clarification. Wild, creative ideas and quantity are desired. Evaluation and the elimination of duplicates take place **after** the brainstorming session has ended. The most promising alternatives are then studied further.

This is an excellent, practical tool for generating creative ideas. It was developed by advertising executive, Dr. Alex Osborn, in the 1930s. It is a particularly useful technique to use with groups. When using brainstorming, groups of people can achieve greater benefit than individuals because of synergism. This means that the product of the group is a multiple, not a sum, of the product of the individuals within the group. The technique centers upon the free flow of ideas. Members of brainstorming groups generate ideas as fast as possible, "rapid fire." at least one member of the group makes a list of the ideas which are described in as few words as possible, usually in one to three words. Evaluation of the ideas takes place later.

5.   **Evaluate the Alternatives**

When evaluating solutions many factors such as cost, labor, resources available, effort involved, affect on morale and other short term and long range effects must be considered. For example, if a solution is extremely expensive to the organization, it may not be practical. But if the basic idea can be kept and a less costly method discovered then the solution may become more feasible. One easy-to-use method for evaluating alternative solutions is to develop a set of evaluation criteria, judgement standards, and then rate each alternative against each criterion.

83

A simple rating 1 to 5 rating scale can be used for this purpose; e.g. 1 = Poor while 5 = Excellent. Alternative solutions are then ranked according to the sum of their scores.

6.   Decide and Act

It should be remembered that whichever method is used to help evaluate alternative solutions there is no substitute for judgement. In many cases two or more alternatives may be ranked so closely that the numerical difference is not significant. Ultimately, the work group leader or the problem solving team must decide which is the best solution and must act to implement it.

Solution implementation requires planning, organizing, communicating, coordinating, follow-up and control -- all components of the management cycle. It also involves anticipating barriers to solution implementation (like apathy, resistance to change, hidden personal agenda and fear) and preparing ways by which those barriers can be overcome.

The follow-up of a solution can take many forms, depending upon all the factors relating to it. It may be a short written report evaluating the solution and its effects. Or, with a very complex decision, the evaluation may be lengthy and detailed. In any event, information must be obtained to measure the effects of the solution.

Problem solving can be accomplished by individual employees within an organization acting alone or it can be done by employees collaboratively in a team environment. The same basic six-step process is followed in either case. However, when employees engage in team problem solving they must also use effective team interaction skills. This means that they must be sure to include and involve all of the team's resources in the problem solving effort. They must use active listening skills, encourage the full participation of all team members and apply the empowerment principle of shared responsibility. Team problem solving is usually more time consuming than solving a problem as an individual contributor. However, team problem solving can be far more effective and the team process enhances commitment to the problem solution.

Problems cannot be solved unless decisions are made. Problem solving and decision making are essentially the same process. Team decisions are affected not only by the extent that a rational decision making (problem solving) process is followed but also by the extent that members of a team share with each other information relevant to the decision issue in an open, candid, honest and trustful manner.

Team members who are more quiet and non-participative by nature must be encouraged to join in the discussion and contribute their ideas. Those who are normally more vocal and participative should certainly take an active role in the discussion but should be careful not to monopolize or control it. When disagreement arises, it should be seen as a constructive way to air different points of view. It is important that team members work in harmony toward a common goal rather than engage in unproductive conflict with each other.

At the same time, the team cannot afford to forget that a job must be done and a decision must be made. They must avoid excessive socializing and must focus on completing the task. This includes ensuring that the decision is made in a timely manner. When a team works collaboratively as discussed above it has a very good chance to achieve synergy.

Activity 8
Solving Problems

Title

    Einstein Paradigm

Time

    About 15-20 minutes

Description

The scenario places participants in the role of members of a national security think tank. The "Secretary" has called an emergency meeting of this team and without explanation wants to know how they would allocate their decision making time if they had only one hour to make a life or death decision! Based on a decision making time allocation process attributed to the late Albert Einstein.

Objective

To familiarize participants with the importance of using a rational process when making decisions or solving problems.

Suitable for

Employees at all organizational levels.

Material

Copies of activity handouts as required for class members and facilitators, note pads with pencils or pens, flip chart with marker.

Best for

Excellent for beginning a decision making skills training session or to reinforce the need to avoid premature "solution finding."

Presentation

1. Divide the group into teams of from 4 to 6 people each. Arrange seating so that the teams are at tables where they can conveniently lay out material and discuss the problem.

2. Distribute one copy of Exhibit 8.1 The Situation for the Einstein Paradigm, which includes instructions, to all team members. Read the Situation to the class aloud. Tell the class that the main purpose of this exercise is to introduce the process by which rational decisions are made. State that they will have only 10 minutes for this activity. During this time they are to list any key points brought out during their team discussion on the flip chart paper that was provided to them.

3. Begin the activity and allow the teams the allotted time to work on it. During that time carefully observe the behavior of the various teams, especially with respect to whether they freely communicate with each other, whether there is full participation in the exercise and the way that they process information and use it to reach a decision.

4. At the end of 10 minutes halt the activity. At random select one or more teams and ask a representative from each to briefly (in 3-5 minutes) present his or her team's findings to the rest of the class. Then, after the selected team(s) has made its presentation distribute handout Exhibit 8.2 to all members of the class. Read Exhibit 8.2 aloud, using the handout as a "lead-in" to a brief discussion about alternative decision making and problem solving methods or into a continuation of the principle subject matter of your training module.

5. Conduct an activity debriefing in which you call on teams at random and ask them diagnostic questions about their team process during the activity. Be sure to get feedback from them regarding their own perceptions about how comfortable communication within their group was and also share with them any observations that you made during the activity.

Exhibit 8.1

The Situation for the Einstein Paradigm

You are a member of a national security think tank. You and the other members of the think tank have been called together by the Secretary to make a decision that can have the most serious consequences for the security of the country. All of the information that you will need to make this decision can be made available to you through electronic means from various government sources almost instantaneously. But you have only one hour to make the decision. For national security reasons no explanation has been given to you as to the reason for the decision making time restraint nor has the actual decision situation been explained to you.

Before you and the other members actually begin, the Secretary wants to know exactly what decision making process steps you will follow and how much time you will allocate to each step or phase of the process. Remember, once you begin the actual decision making process you will have only 60 minutes to reach a decision.

Exhibit 8.2

Einstein Decision Model

One anecdote about the late Dr. Albert Einstein is that he was once asked how he would go about making a life or death decision if he had only 60 minutes to do so. The response attributed to Dr. Einstein is that he would use the first 45 minutes to define the decision issue, set a specific decision making objective and reflect on the facts that he knew about the issue. He would then use the next 10 minutes to determine what the decision alternatives were and to establish criteria by which the various alternatives could be evaluated. In the final 5 minutes Einstein stated that he would evaluate the decision alternatives against the criteria that he had selected and decide which was the best alternative.

The point of this anecdote is that the most noted genius of our time would spend 75% of a critical decision making period in pre-solution finding thinking. Actual solution finding would occur only after he had clearly defined the decision issue (the situation with which he was confronted), set an objective and gathered the facts. The Einstein decision model would then look like this:

> Step 1 -- Define decision issue
> Step 2 -- Set objective
> Step 3 -- Gather facts
> Step 4 -- Develop alternatives
> Step 5 -- Evaluate alternatives
> Step 6 -- Decide and act

Unit 9
Brainstorming Ideas

Thoughts for Discussion

This is an excellent, practical tool for generating creative ideas. It was developed by advertising executive, Dr. Alex Osborn, in the 1930s. It is a particularly useful technique to use with groups. When using brainstorming, groups of people can achieve greater benefit than individuals because of synergism. This means that the product of the group is a multiple, not a sum, of the product of the individuals within the group.

The technique centers upon the free flow of ideas. Members of brainstorming groups generate ideas as fast as possible, "rapid fire" at least one member of the group makes a list of the ideas which are described in as few words as possible, usually in one to three words. Evaluation of the ideas takes place later. There are four tested rules for conducting brainstorming sessions:

- Criticism and evaluation are "out."
- Freewheeling is welcomed.
- Quantity is desired.
- Combination and improvement are sought.

Criticism & Evaluation

The major purpose of brainstorming is to generate a large number of ideas. Creativity and spontaneity will come to a halt if group members start criticizing the ideas. Defensiveness or asking for explanations also will hinder the creative flow. When the group stops its idea generation to talk about the ideas, they leave the brainstorming phase and jump into evaluation. Criticism, evaluation and explanations are deferred until a later time.

Free Wheeling

The more impractical and wild the ideas, the better! The farfetched ideas can "trigger" other ideas among members, which may be more practical in thought or application.

Quantity

The odds are that the greater the number of ideas, the greater the number of useful ideas. This allows exploring all possibilities and deferring the evaluation of ideas. You can avoid explanations by keeping the ideas limited to a one or two-word description. Duplication by other team members doesn't matter, it can be sorted out later.

Combination & Improvement

Build on the ideas of other team members. Ideas can be combined to form a better or different idea. This keeps creativity flowing. A team member can periodically read back the list of ideas already generated in order to stimulate thinking about combinations, expansion or improvement.

Keeping the four rules in mind, you can follow these steps to use the brainstorming process:

1. Appoint a recorder, better yet, two recorders to write down ideas generated. Because ideas are generated "rapid fire" this will ensure that all ideas are recorded.

2. Either state a specific topic to a brainstorm or select several ideas, and have the team rank the topics by voting as to which are most important to discuss. This can be done by the team leader who is responsible for initiating the task function of the group.

3. Team members can begin to verbalize ideas as rapidly as they think of them. If a lull occurs after a period of time, don't evaluate the ideas. Have the recorders(s) read the list. Or, you may wish to list the ideas on a flip chart for easy viewing.

4. As an aid, you also can write on the flip chart the six basic questions: Who? What? Where? When? Why? How? Other idea-spurring words to help members see new connections or relationships to the topic can be "manipulative verbs." Examples are: rearrange, combine, reverse, substitute, separate, add, etc.

Brainstorming can be used to identify both problems and solutions in a department or work group. Possible topics are:

- Actual or potential problems.
- Materials, equipment, or procedures that affect costs, quality or schedules.
- Possible causes of problems.
- Possible solutions.

Activity 9
Brainstorming Ideas

Title

The Indispensable Brick

Purpose

To develop skill in using the brainstorming technique to generate creative ideas.

Description

Participants are assigned to brainstorm creative uses of the common brick.

Time

20 minutes

Resources

Note paper, pencils or pens. Flip chart with pad and marker. Masking tape.

Presentation

1. Before administering this exercise read *Unit 7 Brainstorming - Thoughts for Discussion* thoroughly. If necessary read additional materials about the subject to ensure that you, yourself, understand the brainstorming technique.

2. Divide the class into at least two pairs of teams of 4 to 6 people each and seat them around tables. Distribute 2-3 sheets of flip chart paper to each team together with red, blue and black marker pens. Also, make sure that there are note paper and pencils or pens at each table.

3. Select one half of the pairs of teams and tell them that they are the "A" group. Ask them to step outside the room until you call for them. The remaining pairs of teams are the "B" group and they are to remain in the room.

4. Review the rules for brainstorming with the "B" group. Give them illustrations of elements of the technique like deferred judgement, freewheeling, etc. Also tell the "B"group teams to appoint two recorders for each of their teams. The purpose of having two is that when ideas are "flying fast" they might be generated too fast for one person to record all of them and the second recorder will then serve as a backup.

5. Now call the "A" teams back into the classroom and ask them to take their seats at their assigned tables. Suggest that the "A"Teams appoint a recorder but do not suggest a backup recorder for them.

6. Tell all of the teams that in a moment you will assign them a subject that they are to brainstorm. Inform them that from the moment you state the subject they will have 10 minutes to generate as many ideas as possible about it. Make sure that all teams are ready and then announce that the subject is that they are to brainstorm as many uses of the common brick as possible. Begin timing the activity.

7. At the end of 10 minutes halt the activity. Ask the teams to write their lists on flip chart paper (if they have not already done so). Tell them to arrive at a final list by eliminating any duplicates that might be on their original lists.

8. Now, instruct the teams to count the number of uses of the common brick that each developed. Compare the number of uses that the "A" group teams have with the number generated by the "B" group. The "B" group teams should have benefitted by your briefing about the rules for brainstorming and therefore should have at least 10% to 15% more uses that the "B" group teams. Even if that did not occur (experiential activities are sometimes unpredictable) the entire class will have benefitted from the demonstration of the brainstorming technique in action.

9. Lead a brief group discussion about the subject based on key points in the *Unit 9 Brainstorming - Thoughts for Discussion*. Ask the class to give you examples of how they might use the brainstorming technique in a practical way on the job.

Unit 10
Conducting Meetings

Thoughts for Discussion

Conferences and meetings are common throughout business, industry and government. Almost all of us attend meetings of one type or another. Weekly staff meetings, briefing meetings, safety or grievance committee meetings, seminars, production meetings, town hall meetings, training sessions, family conferences, student conferences and many more types of meetings, large or small, are so common in our everyday lives that we generally accept them as inevitable. The nature and purpose of meetings may vary but they all share one thing in common. People assemble for the purpose of processing and sharing information. And, yet, so many times this most fundamental purpose is not accomplished because of poor conference or meeting participation.

Meeting members should be expected to fully participate and to contribute to the accomplishment of the meeting's objectives to the extent that their ability will allow. This is very important to the success of the meeting and therefore all members who are participating should encourage the full inclusion of all other meeting members during discussion periods. The role of the participant is to participate; to ask questions, to share information (both facts and ideas), to offer suggestions, to disagree and to criticize constructively, and to encourage his or her fellow members to participate in a like manner. But often it is difficult for those who are in the meeting to objectively and accurately critique the quality of meeting participation. One way to do this is by using a conference participation diagram like the one shown in **Exhibit 10.1**.

A conference participation diagram is a graphic depiction of the communication flow that takes place during a meeting over short periods of time. The diagram is prepared by observers who record the communication flow on flip charts or marker boards at randomly selected "cuts" of the meeting that are usually of five minutes duration each. It is easy to prepare the diagram. In **Exhibit 10.1**, circled letters of the alphabet represent meeting participants in the order in which they are seated at a conference table. For the purpose of this illustration **"A"** is designated the meeting leader.

A solid line connecting two participants indicates direct communication from one person to the other. An arrow head shows the direction of communication (from one person to the person at whom the arrow is pointing). Arrow heads at both ends of the solid line indicate that a response was made, i.e., two-way communication. Hash marks next to an arrow head show the frequency of communication from the other party to that person. For example, in **Exhibit 10.1 "A"** might have said "Thank you **"D"** that is a good idea." That would be a direct communication from **"A"** to **"D"** and would be represented by a solid line between the two with an arrow head at **"D's"** end and one hash mark next to the arrow head. Further, in the handout it can be seen that **"A"** spoke to **"D"** eight times and that **"D"** responded to **"A"** five times. Lastly, a dotted line to the center of the group represents an indirect communication from one person to the group as a whole. For example, "Well, how should we begin?" In the handout three indirect communications were made by **"A"** to the group in general. The diagram does not distinguish between statements and questions.

Now, refer again to **Exhibit 10.1**. In the five minute "cut" recorded by the observer it can be seen that the greatest amount of communication was between **A** and **D**. **B** and **C** seem to have engaged in a side conversation. **D** and **C** exchanged one communication each but **D** did not respond to **E**'s communication. **F** did not participate in the discussion at all. There were three indirect communications from **"A"** to the group in general, and so on.

The conference participation diagram is a very useful tool for assessing the extent of participation of members during a meeting or team discussion. It can be used as often as needed to help meeting participants develop a better process of inclusion among all members. You can easily demonstrate the benefits of this tool by conducting this activity as part of your communication skills training program and by encouraging the class to use the process whenever they want to critique the quality of the meetings that they attend.

Exhibit 10.1

Conference Participation Diagram

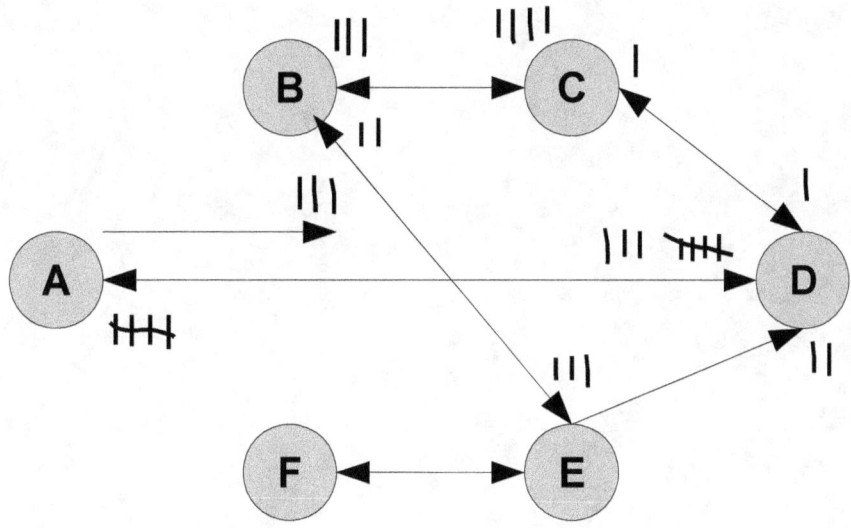

Activity 10
Conducting Meetings

Title

Circles and Arrows

Time

About 35 to 45 minutes

Purpose

The objective of this activity is to demonstrate how the flow of participation during a meeting or conference can be measured and evaluated.

Description

The facilitator instructs the class in the method of constructing a conference participation diagram which is used by observers to chart the flow and frequency of communication among members of a simulated business meeting. A post meeting critique is held to assess the results of the diagram and to help students understand the need for inclusion and active participation by all members of a meeting or conference.

Material

Note pads with pencils or pens for all students and a flip chart with paper and marker. One copy of **Exhibit 10.1** for each member of the class. You will also need to arrange a conference table and seating for six people at the front of the classroom.

Application

Suitable for employees at all organizational levels.

Presentation

1. Distribute one copy of **Exhibit 10.1** to all members of the class. Explain what a conference participation diagram is and how it works.

2. Ask for six volunteers from the class. Give them a simple topic to discuss, one that does not require any special preparation but about which almost anyone will have an opinion, i.e., a sports event, the economy, some recent organization or procedure change at your organization, etc.

3. Appoint a team leader and seat the volunteers at the conference table.

4. Appoint one or more observers and provide them with flip charts. Have them draw circles on the flip charts representing the seating of the volunteers at the table and ask them to write each volunteer's first name in the appropriate circle. Make sure that the observers understand how the diagram is to be drawn during the meeting "cut." Tell the observers to wait at least five minutes into the meeting before they begin to draw the diagram. The purpose of waiting is to allow the communication flow at the table to become more natural and relaxed.

5. Tell the rest of the class that they may join in the activity by constructing their own diagram as they observe the conferees. Then begin the meeting and allow it to proceed for 15 to 20 minutes.

6. At the end of 15 to 20 minutes halt the activity. Instruct the observers to tally the number of hash marks and to report the direction and flow of communication among the meeting participants.

7. Briefly discuss the results of the conference participation diagram with the class. Call attention to any lack of participation or inclusion, any side conversations, and any conversations that dominated others with respect to frequency. Ask the class for their personal observations and any comments that they would like to make about the process.

Bibliography

Axelrod, Alan, Patton on Leadership: Strategic Lessons for Corporate Warfare, Paramus, NJ, Prentice Hall Press, 1999.

Buchholz, Steve and Roth, Thomas (Edited by Karen Hess), Creating The High-Performance Team, New York, John Wiley & Sons, Inc., 1987.

Deeprose, Donna, The Team Coach: Vital New Skills for Supervisors & Managers in a Team Environment, New York, American Management Association, 1995.

Donnellon, Anne, Team Talk: The Power of Language in Team Dynamics, Boston, MA, Harvard Business school Press, 1996.

Harper, Bob and Harper, Ann, Succeeding As A Self-Directed Work Team: 20 Important Questions Answered, Croton-on-Hudson, NY, MW Corporation, 1989.

Kinlaw, Dennis C., Developing Superior Work Teams: Building Quality And The Competitive Edge, San Diego, CA, University Associates, Inc., 1991.

Kinlaw, Dennis C., Team-Managed Facilitation: Critical Skills for Developing Self-Sufficient Teams, San Diego, CA, Pfeiffer & Company, 1992.

Lencioni, Patrick, The Five Dysfunctions of a Team, San Francisco, Jossey-Bass, 2002.

Lewis, James P., Team-Based Project Management, New York, American Management Association, 1998.

Quirk, Thomas L., Successful Team Building, New York, AMACOM, 1992.

Tagliaferri, Louis E., 25 Quick Start Training Activities: To Kick-Off & Energize Your Training Programs, Ponte Vedra Beach, Fl, Talico Developmental Systems L.C., 2010.

Tjosvold, Dean W. And Tjosvold, Mary M., Leading the Team Organization: How to Create an Enduring Competitive Advantage, New York, Lexington Books, 1991.

Appendix A

Tips for Trainers

Tips for Trainers

The purpose of this section is to give you some guidelines and suggestions that can make facilitating the exercises in this series even easier. You can begin by reading this section thoroughly. Remember, your effectiveness as a facilitator will in large part determine the success of your program. Here are some tips that will help to make your job easier:

1. **Commitment**

    The first step in the preparation phase is to ensure that you have the commitment of top management for your training. Management must set the stage by emphatically and enthusiastically expressing its position that the training program is both needed and desirable. Without this endorsement, acceptance and cooperation at lower levels may be only half-hearted.

2. **Time**

    Each of the instructional units in this series is designed to be conducted in 50 minutes or less, including the unit activities. You can extend the time of each exercise as you may choose by adding other Talico material or other material that you might design. Also, you can control the amount of time that you choose to allocate to an exercise by determining how much time you want to devote to introduce the exercise and how much debriefing time you want.

3. **Physical Arrangements**

    a. <u>Where to hold the Training Meeting</u> - Holding training meetings in-house saves money and travel time. On the other hand, being in the plant or office can result in disruptions, such as people being called out to answer the phone or handle problems. Also consider whether in-house facilities are conducive to learning; for example, are they clean, neat, and comfortable? Can the facility supply the audio/visual equipment that you will need? If not, you may want to arrange for course sessions to be held in other facilities. Motels or hotels often have comfortable meeting rooms which can be rented at nominal cost. Your area may have other suitable facilities, as well.

b. <u>The Meeting Room</u> - Wherever you hold the training meeting, you will want to ensure that the room itself is suitable; large enough to accommodate everyone comfortably, well ventilated, heated or air conditioned, and well lit. Also, be sure that the room is located where it is free from distracting noise and make arrangements for any handicapped students.

c. <u>Room Arrangement</u> - You will need tables and chairs for all participants and for the instructor. If you plan to have the participants work on problems in teams, arrange for separate tables for each team. You also will need a table for refreshments, if you provide them.

d. <u>Equipment and Supplies</u> - Be sure to have the required resource material, including pencils and paper for each participant, available for the training session. You may benefit by making overhead transparencies of key learning points developed in your sessions; in which case an overhead projector will also be needed. Also, a flip chart or chalkboard is useful for most sessions.

4. Methods of Instruction

The following alternative presentation methods are discussed for your general interest. It is possible to combine several methods in one session.

a. <u>Lecture</u> - A very common teaching method, this involves the instructor making a one-way presentation to the group. Its advantage is that it involves a high amount of control over the communication process since communication is primarily in one direction, downward. However, one way communication also has certain disadvantages; you receive little feedback from the group and the process by its nature can be a boring method from the group's perspective.

b. <u>Lecturette</u> - This is similar to a lecture but very brief, usually 5-10 minutes in duration. A lecturette can be most effective when used in conjunction with other methods.

c. <u>Group Discussion</u> - This is a very good instructional method for actively involving the class. The leader functions primarily as a catalyst by introducing the subject, using questions to ensure group participation, keeping the discussion on track and, periodically, summarizing and testing for the group's conclusions. Group discussion in conjunction with lecturettes can be an effective mix of teaching methods.

108

d.   <u>Role Playing</u> - Role playing is a proven method by which a person practices a skill he or she is learning. In role playing, each person is assigned a role (either prepared roles or ones that they write themselves) which describes a problem situation and provides information about the character to be played, all relating to the subject of the lesson. Usually two students role play together, one taking the role of an employee and the other that of a supervisor.

The role play participants act out the situation under the observation of their fellow participants. At the conclusion of the brief skit (usually 5-10 minutes), all parties critique the skills demonstrated.

Role playing is especially helpful when the demonstration of a skill will enhance the learning process. Performance appraisal and employee counseling skills are examples of subjects suitable for role playing.

e.   <u>Team Activity</u> - This method is very useful when you want the participants to work together cooperatively to make a decision or solve a problem. First, you should divide the class into teams of from 4 to 6 people each, and seat each team at a separate table. Then, assign problems or situations to each team and let them collectively discuss, analyze, and solve them.

Next, you ask each team to appoint a spokesperson who reports the team's finding and discusses the problem solving or decision making process. This is followed by the rest of the group critiquing the team's work.

There is some question about the optimum size group for this type of activity. As a rule of a thumb, you should not have teams of less than four people each <u>unless</u> you intentionally are setting up diads or triads (teams of two or three, respectively). Teams of less than four people are very easily dominated by only one or two people.

5.   **Activities Overview**

Each exercise begins with a brief synopsis that is designed to provide you with a quick overview of the activity. A **Presentation** section then offers you suggestions for administering the exercise effectively. If you are an experienced platform trainer or facilitator, you may choose to tailor the presentation to your personal instructional style. If facilitating exercises like these is new to you then you will probably benefit by following the presentation guidelines closely. In any event, there is a standard way that you can begin each session.

a.   Read the entire exercise, including all exhibits, thoroughly. Make certain that you understand the learning principles that you want developed by administering the exercise and that you also understand any related technical concept. If you are not entirely clear about these principles, consult the recommended reading list in the appendix or other related material of your own preference.

b.   Begin the exercise session by explaining the purpose of the exercise and the specific learning objectives that you have determined for the group. Present a brief overview of the exercise concept; but be careful not to give away details that might be reserved for only part of the group.

c.   Relate the exercise with the overall training module that you are conducting and explain its part in the learning process. Explain what is meant by experiential learning and tell the group how gaming simulations and role plays facilitate learning. This is necessary because sometimes students find it curious that a "game" is being made part of an instructional program.

d.   Optional: if you are facilitating a session for a large group you may want to appoint one or two co-facilitators who will help you observe and record individual and team behavior during the exercise.

e.   Optional: sometimes a good strategy for using an exercise is to begin without any explanation, administer the exercise, and then after experiential learning has taken place cover the issues in numbers 2 and 3 above. This "shock treatment" approach can be very useful when you want to dramatize certain points.

Appendix B

Presentation Guides

Unit 1 Presentation Guide

Title

    Group Characteristics

Time

    Approximately 1 hour

Objective

To introduce students to basic concepts related to the group process including attributes and characteristics of groups and of people in groups.

Method

Group discussion, lecturette and team activity.

Material

Note pads, pens or pencils, marker board, flip chart with pad and multicolored markers, masking tape and any material suggested in the activity for this unit.

Presentation

1. Introduce yourself as the training facilitator and the welcome the class to this program. Ask the participants to introduce themselves and state their role in the organization, including their length of service.

2. Briefly explain the program's overall purpose and objectives. Give the class an overview of the program content.

3. This entire program is based on experiential learning. The experience that the class will gain from the activity for this unit will serve as an excellent basis for your discussion of unit concepts and will also further serve as an icebreaker.

4. Proceed directly to the activity section for this unit and follow the presentation guidelines for the activity. *Note: the team composition that you assign when you begin the activity should be kept the same for the first five units of this program. Beginning with Unit 6 you can rotate membership of the class among teams as you might feel is appropriate. The reason for this is that in Unit 5 the teams will engage in a self-critique regarding their team performance.*

5. After the activity is completed, including a general debriefing about teamwork and the synergistic benefit of teamwork, conduct a brief lecturette focusing on the unit's key concepts. Follow the lecturette with a general group discussion about the same theme.

6. Ask the class if they have any final questions. If so answer them. Then set a time for the class to meet for the next unit and adjourn the class.

Unit 2 Presentation Guide

Title

    Team Characteristics

Time

    Approximately 50 minutes

Objective

To familiarize students with the distinction between teams and groups.

Method

Group discussion, lecturette and team activity.

Material

Note pads, pens or pencils, marker board, flip chart with pad and multicolored markers, masking tape and any material suggested in the activity for this unit.

Presentation

1.   Briefly review the key concepts and learning points of the previous unit. Ask a few questions of the class to ensure that they understand the concepts and learning points.

2.   Explain the current unit's purpose and objectives. Give the class an overview of the unit's content.

3.   Briefly summarize the principal learning points that you want the students to gain from the current unit. Write those points on a marker board or flip chart. Underline with a marker as may be appropriate.

4. Conduct a group discussion in which you guide the class to distinguish between group and team characteristics but do not go into specific detail (save the detail for the unit activity).

5. Proceed to the activity section for this unit and follow the presentation guidelines for the activity.

6. After the activity is completed conduct a brief lecturette focusing on the unit's key concepts. Follow the lecturette with a general group discussion about the same theme.

7. Ask the class if they have any final questions. If so answer them. Then set a time for the class to meet for the next unit and adjourn the class.

Unit 3 Presentation Guide

Title

Team Functions

Time

Approximately 1 hour

Objective

To acquaint students with the essential task and interpersonal relations functions that must be performed to ensure team effectiveness.

Method

Group discussion, lecturette and team activity.

Material

Note pads, pens or pencils, marker board, flip chart with pad and multicolored markers, masking tape and any material suggested in the activity for this unit.

Presentation

1. Briefly review the key concepts and learning points of the previous unit. Ask a few questions of the class to ensure that they understand the concepts and learning points.

2. Explain the current unit's purpose and objectives. Give the class an overview of the unit's content.

3. Briefly summarize the principal learning points that you want the students to gain from the current unit. Write those points on a marker board or flip chart. Underline with multicolored marker as may be appropriate.

4. State that there are two types of functions that every team must perform in order to ensure team effectiveness. Explain that these are **task** functions and **interpersonal** functions. Lead a group discussion in which you ask the class to develop lists what they believe constitutes examples of both types of functions. Do not arrive at any conclusions at this point but do record their consensus on a flip chart.

5. Proceed to the activity section for this unit and follow the presentation guidelines for the activity.

6. After the activity is completed conduct a brief lecturette focusing on the unit's key concepts. Follow the lecturette with a general group discussion about the same theme.

7. Ask the class if they have any final questions. If so answer them. Then set a time for the class to meet for the next unit and adjourn the class.

Unit 4 Presentation Guide

Title

> **Sharing Information**

Time

> Approximately 1 hour

Objective

> To emphasize and demonstrate to students that information sharing is a key building block of quality team performance.

Method

> Group discussion, lecturette and team activity.

Material

> Note pads, pens or pencils, marker board, flip chart with pad and multicolored markers, masking tape and any material suggested in the activity for this unit.

Presentation

1. Briefly review the key concepts and learning points of the previous unit. Ask a few questions of the class to ensure that they understand the concepts and learning points.

2. Explain the current unit's purpose and objectives. Give the class an overview of the unit's content.

3. Remind the class that this program is based on experiential learning. The experience that the class will gain from the activity will serve as an excellent basis for your discussion of unit concepts and will also further serve as a mid-course energizer.

4. Proceed directly to the activity section for this unit and follow the presentation guidelines for the activity.

5. After the activity is completed conduct a brief lecturette focusing on the unit's key concepts. Place emphasis on the eight strategies listed in *Thoughts for Discussion* that anyone can use immediately to improve his or her team member performance. Follow the lecturette with a general group discussion about the same theme.

8. Ask the class if they have any final questions. If so answer them. Then set a time for the class to meet for the next unit and adjourn the class.

Unit 5 Presentation Guide

Title

Improving Team Performance

Time

Approximately 1 hour

Objective

To further reinforce strategies and techniques for team development and for improving team performance with particular emphasis on continuous improvement.

Method

Group discussion, lecturette and team activity.

Material

Note pads, pens or pencils, marker board, flip chart with pad and multicolored markers, masking tape and any material suggested in the activity for this unit.

Presentation

1. Briefly review the key concepts and learning points of the previous unit. Ask a few questions of the class to ensure that they understand the concepts and learning points.

2. Explain the current unit's purpose and objectives. Give the class an overview of the unit's content.

3. Using the *Thoughts for Discussion* for this unit as a guide, briefly summarize the principal learning points that you want the students to gain from the current unit. Write those points on a marker board or flip chart. Underline with a multicolored marker as may be appropriate.

4. This is the fifth unit in the program. By this time the students will have participated in four experiential learning activities and will now have a basis to assess how effectively they and the other members of their teams performed as a team. The team activity in this unit is especially important because the class will be asked to candidly evaluate how well they are doing as a team and then discuss their critique with the other members of their team.

5. Proceed to the activity section for this unit and follow the presentation guidelines for the activity.

6. After the activity is completed conduct a brief group discussion is which you relate the teams' findings to the main learning points that you had earlier outlined on the marker board or flip chart. You can also relate their findings with the main points in the earlier units.

7. Ask the class if they have any final questions. If so answer them. Inform them that it might be a useful exercise to conduct the *Self-Directed Team Assessment* among the employees of their regular work teams and then use the results for team development and improvement purposes. Then set a time for the class to meet for the next unit and adjourn the class.

Unit 6 Presentation Guide

Title

Leading Teams

Time

Approximately 50 minutes

Objective

To introduce students to the powers, influences and behaviors that enable people to lead others effectively, especially within a team environment.

Method

Group discussion, lecturette and team activity.

Material

Note pads, pens or pencils, marker board, flip chart with pad and multicolored markers, masking tape and any material suggested in the activity for this unit.

Presentation

1. Briefly review the key concepts and learning points of the previous unit. Ask a few questions of the class to ensure that they understand the concepts and learning points.

2. Explain the current unit's purpose and objectives. Give the class an overview of the unit's content.

3. Briefly summarize the principal learning points that you want the students to gain from the current unit. Write those points on a marker board or flip chart. Underline with a multicolored marker as may be appropriate.

4. Conduct a group discussion in which you guide the class to distinguish between group and team characteristics but do not go into specific detail (save the detail for the activity for this unit).

5. Proceed to the activity section for this unit and follow the presentation guidelines for the activity.

6. After the activity is completed conduct a brief lecturette focusing on the unit's key concepts. Follow the lecturette with a general group discussion about the same theme.

7. Ask the class if they have any final questions. If so answer them. Then set a time for the class to meet

Unit 7 Presentation Guide

Title

Collecting Data

Time

Approximately 1.5 hours

Objective

To familiarize students with some of the more common methods and techniques that teams use to collect, process and analyze data.

Method

Group discussion, lecturette and team activity.

Material

Note pads, pens or pencils, marker board, flip chart with pad and multicolored markers, masking tape and any material suggested in the activity for this unit.

Presentation

Note: If you are not familiar with the construction and use of charts and graphs you should take extra time preparing for this unit. Be absolutely sure that you understand all of the unit material before presenting it to the class. Also, in Figure 4 and Exhibit 7.7 the column headed "Cum %" represents a cumulative calculation of percentages of the numbers of items listed relative to the total number of items.

1. Briefly review the key concepts and learning points of the previous unit. Ask a few questions of the class to ensure that they understand the concepts and learning points.

2. Explain the current unit's purpose and objectives. Give the class an overview of the unit's content. Inform the class that this unit presents a considerable amount of technical information and that it might be considered the most difficult unit in the program. However, assure them that the learning issues are very important and that they are well worth the extra effort that the class might have to make in order to master the subject material.

3. Briefly summarize the principal learning points that you want the students to gain from the current unit. Write those points on a marker board or flip chart. Underline with a multicolored marker as may be appropriate.

4. We suggest that you draw replicates of the charts, graphs and tables illustrated in this unit on a marker board or flip chart before class so that you can refer to them during your pre-activity discussion.

5. Proceed to the activity section for this unit and follow the presentation guidelines for the activity.

6. After the activity is completed conduct a brief lecturette focusing on the unit's key concepts. Follow the lecturette with a general group discussion about the same theme.

7. Ask the class if they have any final questions. If so answer them. Then set a time for the class to meet for the next unit and adjourn the class.

Unit 8 Presentation Guide

Title

> **Solving Problems**

Time

> Approximately 1 hour

Objective

> To familiarize students with a 6-step rational method for solving problems and making decisions.

Method

> Group discussion, lecturette and team activity.

Material

> Note pads, pens or pencils, marker board, flip chart with pad and multicolored markers, masking tape and any material suggested in the activity for this unit.

Presentation

1. Briefly review the key concepts and learning points of the previous unit. Ask a few questions of the class to ensure that they understand the concepts and learning points.

2. Explain the current unit's purpose and objectives. Give the class an overview of the unit's content.

3. Briefly summarize the principal learning points that you want the students to gain from the current unit. Write those points on a marker board or flip chart. Underline with a multicolored marker as may be appropriate.

4. Conduct a group discussion about the difference between solving a problem and making a decision. Point out that all problem solving requires decision making, also. Tell the class that the only real difference between problem solving and decision making is that problem solving deals with something that has happened in the past but decision making deals with something that will happen in the future, i.e., the solution to the problem.

5. Proceed to the activity section for this unit and follow the presentation guidelines for the activity.

6. After the activity is completed conduct a brief lecturette focusing on the unit's key concepts. Follow the lecturette with a general group discussion about the same theme.

7. Ask the class if they have any final questions. If so answer them. Then set a time for the class to meet for the next unit and adjourn the class.

Unit 9 Presentation Guide

Title

Brainstorming Ideas

Time

Approximately 1 hour

Objective

To introduce students to the brainstorming method for generating creative ideas.

Method

Group discussion, lecturette and team activity.

Material

Note pads, pens or pencils, marker board, flip chart with pad and multi-colored markers, masking tape and any material suggested in the activity for this unit.

Presentation

1. Briefly review the key concepts and learning points of the previous unit. Ask a few questions of the class to ensure that they understand the concepts and learning points.

2. Explain the current unit's purpose and objectives. Give the class an overview of the unit's content.

3. Briefly summarize the principal learning points that you want the students to gain from the current unit. Write those points on a marker board or flip chart. Underline with multi-colored marker as may be appropriate.

4. Conduct a group discussion that focuses on the subject of creativity. Place emphasis on the value of "thinking outside of the box." Ask the class to give

examples of what they have found in their experience to be barriers to creativity. Discuss how those barriers can be removed.

5. Proceed to the activity section for this unit and follow the presentation guidelines for the activity.

6. After the activity is completed conduct a brief lecturette focusing on the unit's key concepts. Follow the lecturette with a general group discussion about the same theme.

7. Ask the class if they have any final questions. If so answer them. Then set a time for the class to meet for the next unit and adjourn the class.

Unit 10 Presentation Guide

Title

Team Characteristics

Time

Approximately 1.5 hours

Objective

To demonstrate a way for meeting participants to critique how effectively team meetings are being conducted and to provide graphic feedback to teams that can be used to improve the quality of their meetings.

Method

Group discussion, lecturette and team activity.

Material

Note pads, pens or pencils, marker board, flip chart with pad and multicolored markers, masking tape and any material suggested in the activity for this unit.

Presentation

Note: This unit will likely require additional preparation on your part. You may want to prepare sample conference participation diagrams on a marker board or flip chart before class.

1. Briefly review the key concepts and learning points of the previous unit. Ask a few questions of the class to ensure that they understand the concepts and learning points.

2. Explain the current unit's purpose and objectives. Give the class an overview of the unit's content.

3. Briefly summarize the principal learning points that you want the students to gain from the current unit. Write those points on a marker board or flip chart. Underline with a multicolored marker as may be appropriate.

4. Conduct a group discussion centering on the general ineffectiveness of many meetings. Ask the class to volunteer reasons why some meetings they attend might be considered a waste of time. Make a list of those reasons and then group them by categories or types. Discuss what can be done to eliminate or minimize those barriers to meeting effectiveness.

5. Proceed to the activity section for this unit and follow the presentation guidelines for the activity.

6. After the activity is completed conduct a brief lecturette focusing on the unit's key concepts. Follow the lecturette with a general group discussion about the same theme.

7. Ask the class if they have any final questions. If so answer them. Then set a time for the class to meet for the next unit and adjourn the class.

NOTES

www.ingramcontent.com/pod-product-compliance
Lightning Source LLC
Chambersburg PA
CBHW081130170526
45165CB00008B/2612